It was an archaeological and architectural project of monumental proportions – and a project in which the quest for accuracy was often considered less important than the quest for beauty. On this page and the pages following are coloured drawings by Louis Duc, Jacques Carlu, Constant Moyaux and Ferdinand Dutert.

TEMPLE DE LA CONCORDE

TEMPLE DE VESPASIEN

TABULARIUM

MONT

CAPITOL

SATVRNE

TEMPLE DE SATVRNE

ROCHE TARPEIENNE

CONTENTS

IN SEARCH OF
ANCIENT ROME

Claude Moatti

THAMES AND HUDSON

12

In spite of being destroyed and buried time and time again over the centuries, Rome never disappeared entirely. The Eternal City – a great intellectual, political and artistic capital – has survived, though the veil of legend has covered its ruins.

CHAPTER 1
ROME, THE ETERNAL CITY

The *Dittamondo,* by the 14th-century author Fazio degli Uberti, is an account of an imaginary voyage. Fazio and his guide, the ancient geographer Solinus, arrive at the banks of a river, where they encounter an old, weeping woman (opposite, detail); she is Rome, the city personified, and she tells the poet her story and about her former beauty.

Right: a 5th-century personification of Rome.

As in so many other ancient cities, Rome's history has been obscured. Even in ancient times, buildings were constructed on top of each other: the Baths of Trajan were built over the ruins of the Domus Aurea or Golden House of Nero; the Baths of Diocletian were built on top of two temples and several public and private buildings.

Strolling through the city in the 16th century, the French philosopher and essayist Michel de Montaigne remarked that he knew he was walking 'over the roofs of entire houses' and 'on top of the old walls'.

Two centuries later the German poet Johann Wolfgang von Goethe (1749–1832) walked through the Campo Vaccino noting that the ancient Roman Forum, surrounded by all kinds of buildings, had become cow pasture; here and there half-buried ruins

F. Chauveau fe.

appeared. (Archaeologists would not clear it until the following century.)

'The hills rise above the rubble', wrote Frontinus, the administrator of the aqueducts in the 2nd century AD. Before the end of the Roman Empire in the 5th century, the physical remains of earlier epochs – royal Rome and republican Rome – had already practically disappeared, covered by more recent construction, which in turn was destined to meet with a similar fate.

For over a thousand years, since the end of the empire, ancient Roman remains have been re-emerging gradually from layers of rubble and soil more than 20 m thick in some places.

In the 12th century, when the struggle between the empire and the papacy had reached its height, the traditional belief that the Emperor Constantine had offered the empire to Pope Sylvester – thereby giving him a legitimate foundation for the political power of the popes – was revived. A series of 12th-century frescoes in the Oratory of St Sylvester illustrates this event: in this example (opposite) Constantine is presenting the crown to the pope.

For much of the city's history, Romans were the conquerors (left, a 17th-century illustration). When Alaric the Visigoth and his tribe of migrating barbarians arrived in 410 AD, however, it was the citizens of Rome who suffered. The city never recovered its glory.

CIRCI MAXIMI et PALATII MAIORIS
ut hodie visuntur RELIQVIÆ.

PIRAMIS AVT SEPVLCHRVM C·CESTII·PROPE PORTÃ S·PAVLI

Rome robbed of its treasures: Rome destroyed

Burial was not the only way ancient Roman architectural
treasures disappeared. The city's riches were also
forcibly removed. In the 4th century AD Rome was losing
its status as capital of the empire. The new capitals,
Constantinople, and later Milan and Ravenna, were
each in turn adorned with Rome's riches, taken by
the emperors. General impoverishment and invasions by

Germanic and other groups accelerated the damage. The inhabitants no longer kept up the buildings, the statues and cult objects that were spared by the invaders were dispersed, and the ancient sites – the Forum, the Palatine Hill, the Colosseum – gradually became public refuse dumps or became overgrown or covered with the débris of time.

Some rulers and some invaders, however, were impressed with the monuments that were still visible and attempted to protect them. The Eastern Roman Emperor Constantius II, son of Constantine the Great, who would himself strip Rome of a large number of bronzes, was overwhelmed when he made a pilgrimage to the Eternal City in 357. He was fascinated by Trajan's Forum, with its sculpted column and its basilica, and its markets that stood on the slopes of the Quirinal Hill. He felt that he was looking at 'the sanctuary of the world'. Theodoric I, king of the Visigoths and ruler of Italy in the late 5th century AD, had Pompey's Theatre repaired and encouraged the restoration of the baths, circuses (arenas), sewers, and aqueducts.

From the pagan city to the Christian city: pillage and re-use

After the conversion of the Emperor Constantine around AD 312, Rome became Christian. Pagan worship was banned, and temples were closed by decree at the end of the 4th century. Some temples eventually became churches: the Pantheon, built by Agrippa

Opposite: the Circus Maximus in a 17th-century engraving (above); the Pyramid of Cestius, a funerary monument built at the end of the 1st century BC (below); and a cross section of Trajan's Column (right) – both the latter seen in 16th-century engravings. Left: Trajan's Column.

The opening to the sky in the dome of the Pantheon (below) measures 9 m across. Bottom: the Pantheon in a 17th-century drawing.

The drawings of Maerten van Heemskerck were produced between 1532 and 1536, following Charles V's sack of Rome. The artist has become a precise and realistic observer: he does not guess about the former state of the monuments or invent a reconstruction. The Colosseum really did look like this in the 16th century (though Heemskerck ornaments the foreground with extra sculptures).

(son-in-law of Augustus, the first Roman emperor), was consecrated as early as 609 to St Mary of the Martyrs; the Curia – where the senate met, in the Forum – was dedicated to St Adrian.

The urban landscape at large was rapidly being transformed. Exhausted by wars, famines, and epidemics, people had abandoned the hills and taken refuge along the Tiber. For several centuries Rome's densely populated centre was surrounded by vast abandoned spaces overgrown with vegetation.

Finally, beginning in the 11th century, the ancient buildings that were still intact were taken over and fortified by noble families. The others – temples, baths and theatres in varying states of disrepair – were used as quarries for marble, an invaluable building material, which all too often was merely burned to produce lime. In fact, throughout the Middle Ages, until the Renaissance, thousands of statues and fragments of marble were burned in smoky limekilns set up between the Capitoline Hill and the Tiber: a street name there has preserved the memory of the destruction – the Via delle Botteghe Oscure, the 'street of dark shops'.

In the 19th century the archaeologist Rodolfo Lanciani (1847–1929) uncovered limekilns in the Forum, located on site, as it were, which made them most efficient. On the Palatine Hill he found a ditch full of statues, 'some charred, others intact', that had been spared for some unknown reason. When it was not burned, the marble of the statues, wall facings and columns was sent to Naples, Pisa, Orvieto, Monte Cassino, St-Denis in France, or even Westminster Abbey in England.

All this plunder gave the ruins their present appearance. During the empire Rome had been a city of gleaming marble.

For pilgrims Rome was the most important of all cities, the centre of the world. The map below, from the *Einsiedeln Itinerary,* portrays the city as a perfect circle and illustrates the more famous routes. The most important one goes from the Vatican, upper left, across the river to the Lateran, bottom.

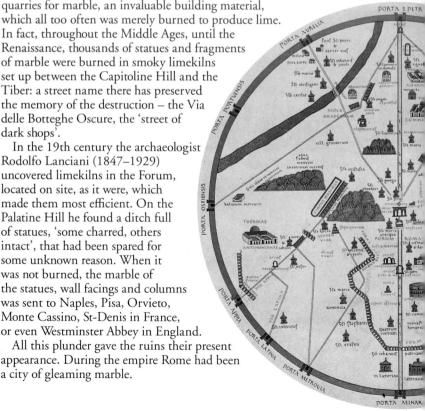

Rome reborn again and again

Yet the buried and broken city never disappeared completely. The Colosseum, the Pantheon and Trajan's Column have endured through the centuries. Rome has always retained a breath of life, and its 'rebirths' were suffused with emotion. In spite of the hostility of the Christians to paganism, the study of Roman history and traditions was not interrupted from the 1st century BC until the Middle Ages. Even then a familiarity with the ancient culture survived in some quarters, and its ruins were viewed with profound respect.

Nicolas Poussin's drawing of the statue of Marcus Aurelius.

The earliest guides to Rome mention the pagan monuments

Christian Rome attracted visitors from other parts of Europe just as pagan Rome had. Crowds of pilgrims came to visit the tomb of St Peter (located in what was originally Nero's Circus), the churches containing the relics of other saints, and the ancient ruins close by. More than two million came in 1300, the jubilee year, when it had been rumoured that anyone who visited St Peter's would receive full absolution.

Guides written specially for these travellers to Rome proposed various tours. One of the oldest and most famous of these, dating from the 8th or the 9th century and known as the *Einsiedeln Itinerary* (because the manuscript was discovered in the Einsiedeln monastery in

"In front of the pope's palace, the Lateran, there is a bronze statue: the horse is huge, and his rider, whom some people think is Theodoric, is believed by Romans to be the Emperor Constantine; for the cardinals and the clerics of the Roman Curia, however, he is Marcus or Quintus Quirinus.... The rider is sitting erect; he is leading the people with his right hand and holding the reins in his left hand."

Magister Gregory

MIRABILIA
URBIS ROMAE NOVA
rercognita et emendata aña
in verum sensum
reducta.

Anno Iubilei.   M. D. L.

RO MA.

Switzerland), offers pilgrims eleven walks through the city. It gives a detailed description of the city walls, enumerating the towers, crenellations, windows, and even latrines.

The *Einsiedeln Itinerary* combines a sound knowledge of the city with a special interest in the inscriptions – texts that the ancients engraved on monuments. (The study of inscriptions was a major field in the renewal of classical studies which, as a result of Charlemagne's influence, was taking place at the time.)

The title page of a *Mirabilia* produced for the jubilee year of 1550 (left).

The *Mirabilia,* the cult books of medieval tourism

The *Einsiedeln Itinerary* was only one of many guides for pilgrims called *Mirabilia Urbis Romae* (*Marvels of Rome*) which had been published for centuries. By the 12th century the *Mirabilia* reflected a decline in the understanding of the city. Direct knowledge of texts and places was obscured by legends and symbols.

Antiquity had acquired a mythological dimension; the ancients appeared to be inimitable giants who had adorned their city with the greatest wonders. In the 12th century Canon Benedict, a cleric at St Peter's while Innocent II was pope, described these extraordinary works to his contemporaries. By studying ancient texts, Benedict attempted to find the ancient names of the monuments; these names had long been obscured by medieval nomenclature. But his commentary included all the legends and errors of the Middle Ages: he wrote, for example, that the demigods Castor and Pollux were 'two young philosophers who had come to Rome in the time of Tiberius', and that, in the Forum, 'there is the Temple of Vesta, beneath which it is said that a dragon lies'. He imagined that marvellous palaces resplendent with gold and silver had stood on the Capitoline Hill.

In the 12th century the Romans were demanding their independence from the papacy; while the popes and the Germanic emperors conceived competing plans for a universal Roman-style empire with Rome as its centre, the Romans dreamed of an Italy united under them, a new republic built on the pattern of the ancient one. The ancients were admired as highly as ever, and their influence continued to grow.

The *Mirabilia* reflected the desire of the time to revive the consuls and senators, hoping to resuscitate the splendour of the city. These books were very popular. Copied again and again, distributed and imitated until the 16th century, they set the style of topographical description for a long time to come and gave a lasting account of what was known about Roman monuments. In the 14th century the Italian poet Petrarch derived all that he knew about the city from these guides.

Magister Gregory, enamoured of Venus

Among the most famous *Mirabilia*, the work of Magister Gregory holds a special place: an English theologian, Gregory was a true lover of antiquity who did not hesitate to criticize destructive and iconoclastic popes. When he arrived in Rome he was fascinated from the very first glimpse by this city's many towers, narrow streets, and innumerable churches. The walks he took increased his admiration: he saw pyramids, arches and monumental buildings. He

Left: in the Middle Ages some people believed that this colossal head of the Emperor Constantine represented the sun-god.

Above: the Emperor Frederick II (1194–1250) was extremely knowledgeable about ancient Rome, and he encouraged Classical studies. In Sicily he established the first medieval codification of the administrative laws of state, which were inspired by the Roman code of the Emperor Justinian.

was delighted by everything, especially the statues. Their beauty seemed to him to come from a magical power. One in particular fascinated him, a Venus 'which is so indescribably perfect that she almost seems to be alive; like a girl blushing at her own nudity, her face grows red.' Gregory went back to see her three times, in spite of the long walk he had to take to get there.

Gregory was not a scholar, even though he claims that he was not taken in by all the stories pilgrims were generally told. But he lived in the Middle Ages, and his observations reflect a time when Rome had become a confusing labyrinth, a forest in which travellers could get lost. It was a time when a taste for legends had taken the place of every other form of understanding. The Pantheon was believed to have been the home of demons; the Colosseum, the Temple of the Sun. But Gregory also pointed the way to 14th-century humanism, both by his sense of pure beauty and by his ability to be moved by a statue.

A time of tension and turmoil

This was a period of tension, marked by a series of challenges to papal authority. In 1309 Philip IV of France forced the relocation of the papacy to Avignon. During the popes' exile, which lasted until 1378, most Italian cities were experiencing a strong national awakening stimulated by a revival of interest in ancient culture.

The political renaissance of Rome seemed to favour archaeological research: excavations were organized, and vases, pottery and statues found at various sites increasingly attracted attention. The Emperor Frederick II (who ruled from 1215 to 1250) organized the exploration of the ancient Greek city near Augusta, the city he had founded in 1232. Of course, people's interest in marbles and statues during this period was primarily to trade in them. Admirers of antiquities were treasure hunters, and the respect for some works, especially tall bronze statues, was partly motivated by the inability to make similar ones at the time.

Cola di Rienzo, Tribune of the People, and the nostalgia for Republican Rome

A young Roman by the name of Cola di Rienzo (1313–54), who was a friend of Petrarch and a defender of the people against the abuses of the nobles, 'spent whole days examining the marble

NICOLO DI LORENZO DETTO COLA DI RENZO, Tribuno del Popolo Romano.

sculptures that littered the ground in Rome', according to his anonymous biographer. Apparently, no-one could read the ancient epitaphs as well as Cola di Rienzo: he could explicate all the ancient inscriptions and interpret correctly all the marble figures.

In 1346 Rienzo discovered a bronze plaque engraved with the law bestowing imperial powers on the Emperor Vespasian (ruler from AD 69 to 79). It had been re-used in the altar of the Lateran Basilica, built probably in the 4th century. For centuries, the inscription had faced inwards. A fire in the basilica finally led to its discovery and deciphering.

Rienzo displayed the document and assembled the people. Already well known for his anti-aristocratic feelings, he explained: 'Sublime Rome lies in the dust, she cannot see her own fall since the emperor and the pope have torn her two eyes out. Romans, see how great was the magnificence of the senate that conferred the

If the 14th-century Italian poet Petrarch (opposite, painted by Andrea del Castagno) was to be considered by posterity to be the incarnation of the renewal of Classical literature, Cola di Rienzo (above) represents the desire to revive the political forms of antiquity. Later he became a tyrant and finally was killed during a popular uprising. He was dragged through the streets of the city for three whole days; his body was beaten, stoned, dismembered and then burned.

empire on this individual!'

The people of Rome listened attentively. In 1347 Rienzo was elected Tribune of the People. He spoke on the very spot where the Gracchi, Cicero and the Caesars had once aroused the crowds' passions.

But this 'liberator' who exalted the people, this defender of the communal ideal who reduced the barons to impotence, reformed the city-state, and strove for Italian unity, slowly became a terrible tyrant. He was deposed and imprisoned. When he was called back to resume his authority, his excesses became even more outrageous. Finally, he was tortured and put to death.

From the scholars of the Middle Ages to the Renaissance humanists

Rienzo's learning was considerable, and he had a great understanding of the monuments, literary texts and inscriptions; but he was the last person of his time to call for the political restoration of Rome.

His contemporary Giovanni Dondi, a philosopher, physician and astrologer, already belonged to the age of humanism. In Dondi's *Iter Romanum*, a collection of notes made on a journey to Rome, he gives the precise dimensions of the monuments and avoids repeating mere legends.

Dondi's approach to antiquity is unemotional: he does not appeal to magic, to political exaltation, or to poetry. His encounter with Rome relies on figures and texts. His admiration is the product of a critical mind.

This 1st-century bronze tablet conferring imperial powers on Vespasian was discovered by Cola di Rienzo in 1346 in the Lateran Basilica.

A late 13th-century drawing (opposite) portrays Rome in the form of a lion. Rienzo noted: 'The walls of the city form the outline of a lion at rest.'

While Christopher Columbus was exploring the New World, artists, scholars, princes, adventurers and popes were searching feverishly through the soil of Rome for the remains of its former splendour. Rome was being plundered; brought back to life in descriptions, maps and plans; and actually rebuilt – all at the same time.

CHAPTER 2
THE AGE OF THE HUMANISTS

The *Laocoön* (opposite, in a room in the Domus Aurea, where it was discovered) is 'an artistic wonder, in which the greatest beauty is born of the greatest suffering', according to the 18th-century German archaeologist Johann Joachim Winckelmann.

This map of Rome comes from the Limbourg brothers' *Très Riches Heures du Duc de Berry* (15th century).

In the 15th century the city was dirty, depopulated, and completely in ruins; a contemporary description compared it to an old woman dressed in rags. The great historian Gian Francesco Poggio Bracciolini (1380–1459) saw in Rome the symbol of humanity, subject as it was to the vagaries of fortune.

In what was a genuine challenge to time, antiquarians, those learned in ancient matters, undertook to restore both the city's identity and its unity.

In addition, great projects to care for public works were organized by the popes. Because of their overwhelming passion for collecting masterpieces from the pagan past, the popes were even accused of heresy on the eve of the sack of Rome by the troops of Charles V in 1527.

More than anything else, however, it was the insatiable intellectual fervour of the period that was responsible for the beginnings of archaeological research. As the great explorers set sail for new continents, scholars, artists and princes set off in search of Rome.

Four drawings from the 15-century *Codex Mutinesis*. Above left: Monte Testaccio, an artificial hill formed of fragments of pottery, marking an ancient commercial site. Above: an imaginative view of the Lateran, showing the statue of Marcus Aurelius and the hand and head of a colossal statue, enhancing the power of the Lateran as a place of justice and the political power of the popes. At the end of the 15th century and the beginning of the 16th, these bronze sculptures were moved to the Capitol, where they remain to this day.

Scholarly walks

Cyriacus of Ancona (1391–1452), a merchant and dealer in antiquities, rode his white horse through the city every day 'in search of remains, temples, theatres, palaces, and baths, splendid obelisks, arches, aqueducts, bridges, statues, columns, and noble inscriptions. He examined them, transcribed them, and commented upon them'; he wanted to revive the dead and reveal their identity. In his *Itinerary*, he tells of his expeditions to Italy, Egypt, Greece, and Palestine. He includes copies of numerous previously unpublished texts and drawings of many monuments.

Like Cyriacus, other scholars of the period were enthusiastic explorers. Flavio Biondo and Poggio Bracciolini ventured to the outskirts of Rome; Julius Pomponius Laetus (1425–98), like Dondi a century earlier, collected the notes he took in the course of his walks and produced one of the best topographical commentaries of his time.

Symbols of Rome are placed among imaginary monuments and antiquities. Above left: an obelisk with a globe in front of a building that combines the basilican form of old St Peter's with the angel-topped rotunda of the Castel Sant' Angelo. Above right: a view outside the walls, with a fortified bridge over the Tiber.

Philology's finest hour

The scholars' passion for exploration was directed first toward manuscripts. These learned people travelled all over Europe, searching monasteries for them and copying and translating the texts they found. Pope Nicholas V (who reigned from 1447 to 1455) never went anywhere without his army of scribes. At the time of the fall of Constantinople, Nicholas ordered his agents to acquire Greek manuscripts regardless of their cost. For the eight years of his papacy, he expanded the collections of the Vatican Library, which, with its five thousand volumes, became the first great library of Europe. His scholars, including Poggio Bracciolini, began to translate and explicate texts in order to establish sound editions from the variants found in different manuscripts.

One of the reading rooms of the Vatican Library at the beginning of the 17th century (above).

Among the Roman authors rediscovered at the time were Ovid, Livy, Lucretius, Statius, Quintilian and, most significantly, the 1st-century writer Vitruvius. Vitruvius' treatise, *De Architectura,* would influence both the architecture of the Renaissance – for example, in the work of Andrea Palladio (1508–80) – and the understanding of the ancient monuments. Using Vitruvius, and also mathematical instruments he himself had invented, the architect Leon Battista Alberti (1404–72) measured the ancient buildings and produced precise drawings of them. His *Description of Rome,* copiously illustrated with drawings and measurements, includes not only descriptions of monuments but analyses of their structure.

This illuminated manuscript of Livy's *History of Rome* dates from the 14th century.

"Among the copyists, those who knew Greek occupied the first rank; there were only a few of them and they were paid well.... At the time of Nicholas V, most of the copyists in Rome were Germans and Frenchmen: they were called barbarians by the Italian humanists."

Jacob Burckhardt (1818–97), *The Civilization of the Renaissance in Italy*

Saving the memory of stone

Philology, the study of ancient language and literature, went hand in hand with a systematic search for inscriptions – dedications of monuments, funerary texts, laws, and *senatus consulta* (decrees of the Roman senate). Bernardo Rucellai's work *De Urbe Roma,* for example, brought descriptions and inscriptions together. Scholars hurriedly made tremendous efforts to save the memory made of stone, with a haste and passion reflecting their legitimate fear of seeing its last traces disappear, as new monuments were still being built with stones taken from the old ones. In 1430 Poggio Bracciolini began a series of

Opposite: for centuries Venus had occupied a very important place in the Roman pantheon. Rome did not become a divinity protecting the empire until the reign of the Emperor Hadrian (AD 117–38). At that time the twin Temple of Venus and Rome – with its two apsed sanctuaries and its colonnades that dominated both the Forum and the Colosseum – was regarded as the religious and political centre of the state. By the 15th century the building was a ruin; this drawing of it by Andrea Palladio shows an idealized view rather than an archaeological reconstruction.

Tempio di O. et D

sylloges – collections of pagan and Christian inscriptions. *Sylloges* proliferated in subsequent centuries with the help of the printing press and the enthusiasm of numerous publishers.

All these collections, which scholars in the 18th and 19th centuries took the trouble to classify, reveal a widely shared determination to bring together as many documents as possible. The haste of collecting caused some problems: the dates of discoveries were often not noted; places where fragments were found, and their dimensions, were often not recorded. Sometimes data were entirely invented.

Humanist scholarship – a heresy?

In his house on the Quirinal Hill, Julius Pomponius Laetus amassed inscriptions, coins and fragments of marble; together with his friends and disciples he founded the Roman Academy, an association of enthusiasts and scholars. At their meetings they ate sumptuous banquets in the ancient style. Sometimes they assembled in the catacombs (subterranean burial vaults of the Early Christians), where one can still find the graffiti they left. Every member assumed an ancient name: Pomponius took the name of Pontifex Maximus,

which was both the title of the head of the Roman religion in ancient times and the Latin term for 'pope'.

When word of their meetings reached Pope Paul II, he became worried that Pomponius was a heretic who was organizing pagan banquets for his friends. Was he plotting some kind of conspiracy? In 1468 twenty members of the society were arrested and put in chains in the

Originally the mausoleum of the Emperor Hadrian, the Castel Sant' Angelo (above, with the flag) was transformed into a fortress in the 3rd century AD, when it was incorporated into the great Aurelian Wall. Its defences were continually reinforced until the 16th century. During the sack of Rome in 1527 Pope Clement VII took refuge there by using the fortified corridor that linked it with the Vatican.

Adversaries Julius Pomponius Laetus (left above), an Italian humanist, and Pope Paul II (left below).

dungeon of the Castel Sant' Angelo. Pomponius wrote a defence and protested his innocence. What followed was one of the first trials in modern history in which humanist scholarship was equated with paganism. It prefigured the accusations that were made against the church a century later during the Reformation.

There was no proof of the guilt of the scholars, who were nonetheless accused of every vice. (The meetings in the catacombs and the graffiti remained secrets.) Pomponius was released. Immediately, he resumed his lectures at the university, and they were so popular that students arrived before midnight to reserve their seats. Pope Sixtus IV, who succeeded Paul II in 1471, even allowed Pomponius to revive the Academy, which was later joined by a large number of scholars, including the statesman Baldassare Castiglione and Cardinal Pietro Bembo. Finally, however, the sack of Rome in 1527 led to the dissolution of the too-pagan Academy.

The birth of literary topography

Pomponius' knowledge of the ancient monuments placed him among the greatest experts in this field at a time that saw the rise of topography, the analysis of the structures and features of the ancient city. In the 15th century attempts were made to restore the ancient place names that had been obscured by the Middle

At times, ancient literary texts and inscriptions support each other: the bronze tablet below, discovered in 1528, reproduces Claudius' speech to the Roman senate on behalf of the Gauls; it served to corroborate Tacitus' account of the speech in his *Annals,* written a century later.

Ages, and to rediscover the reality that lay behind the
medieval legends. Poggio Bracciolini, Bernardo Rucellai,
and especially Flavio Biondo were the first to compare
texts with inscriptions and remains. The very title of
Biondo's book *Roma Instaurata* (*Rome Restored*) revealed
the aim of these new topographers: to rebuild Rome by
scholarly evocation, which was just as important as
physical restoration. Biondo's second book, *Roma
Triumphans*, was a treatise on Roman antiquities. He
loved the ruins and he admired modern and Christian –
'triumphant' – Rome, whose greatness seemed to him to
extend that of the ancient city.

For the topographers of the 15th century, ancient
literature was more important than any other source.
Archaeology was not yet a science. There were no

"The artist may be
inspired by wild
flowers,...or by other
motifs that are called
grotesques.... This name
does not suit them, since
ancient artists enjoyed
imagining monsters that
combined the forms of
goats, cows and mares, or
by mingling different
forms of foliage, they
created different types of
monsters. Monsters is, in
fact, their true name, and
it suits them much better
than grotesques."
Benvenuto Cellini
(1500–71)
Autobiography

Grotesques by
assistants of Raphael
in the Vatican Logge,
c. 1517–9, modelled on
ancient Roman
decorations.

scientific excavations, only individuals rummaging about
looking for treasures in the soil. The only written
accounts of major discoveries were produced by amateurs

and were only picturesque catalogues devoid of historical analysis. Similarly, artists were looking for models. They depicted ruins in the state in which they found them rather than excavations in progress. It was not until the end of the 16th century that the first reliable accounts of excavations began to appear.

This drawing of a richly painted vault in the Domus Aurea is by Pietro Santi Bartoli, a 17th-century artist.

Roman artists discover the 'grotesques' of the Domus Aurea

At the beginning of the 16th century, labourers working near the Colosseum penetrated a buried building whose vaults were adorned with frescoes and stuccos. This was the Domus Aurea or Golden House, a huge palace built by the Emperor Nero (ruled 54–68 AD) over the remains of a building that had burned down. The Domus Aurea had burned in its turn and had been covered over by the Baths of Trajan. It was some time before the imperial residence was identified.

The Domus Aurea galleries, which were thought to have been underground from the very beginning, were called 'grottoes', and their mural paintings of ornamental designs and mythological figures were called 'grotesques'. The discovery of the grotesques was to have a profound

Julius II, pope from 1503 to 1513, shown here in a portrait by Raphael, claimed descent from the family of Julius Caesar.

The discovery of the *Laocoön* (below) in 1506 affected all artists, who eagerly copied what they considered to be *the* masterpiece of ancient art. This mid-16th-century drawing (left) is by Federico Zuccari. Recent discoveries made at Sperlonga, south of Rome, suggest that the *Laocoön* is not an original Roman statue but a marble copy of a Hellenistic work made of bronze.

influence on the artists of the Renaissance, who began to decorate palaces with imitations of them. One of the greatest, Raphael (1483–1520), also drew inspiration from them when decorating the Logge in the Vatican Palace. Even more important was the fact that the frescoes provided the first colour illustrations of antiquity: the mural paintings of Pompeii and Herculaneum were not discovered until two centuries later.

The *Laocoön,* 'the masterpiece of the arts', arouses everyone's desire

The Domus Aurea contained inexhaustible riches. In 1547 alone twenty-five statues were discovered there; but the greatest discovery had been made

earlier, in 1506, when the owner of the land found a
sculptural group representing two children and their
father in the grip of a serpent: this was the *Laocoön*,
which Pliny the Elder (AD 23–79) had called the
masterpiece of the arts. Sent to inspect it by Pope
Julius II, both the architect Giuliano da Sangallo
(1445–1516) and Michelangelo (1475–1564) confirmed
Pliny's judgment. This marvellous work seemed, as a
contemporary wrote, 'to exude the scent of
immortality'. Pope Julius acquired it and had it
moved to the Belvedere Court in the Vatican, in what
was truly a triumphant procession.

The fame of the
Laocoön became so
great that, after the
Victory of Marignano
in 1515, Francis I, the
king of France, claimed it
as one of his spoils of war.
Pope Leo X (Julius'
successor in 1513) refused
to part with the
original and
secretly had a
copy of it made;
but neither the
original nor the
copy ever reached
the French king.

Much later, in 1797, the *Laocoön* was carried off
by Napoleon as a spoil of war, but it was restored to
the Vatican after his defeat.

The first collections of antiquities are kept at the Belvedere Court and on the Capitoline Hill

The *Laocoön* joined another pagan statue at the
Belvedere, an exquisite Apollo. Leo X added others
that were found behind the Pantheon. The collection
thus grew rapidly, in spite of the reluctance expressed
by some popes to acquire ancient pagan art. Adrian
VI (1522–3) and Pius V (1566–72), for example,
were hostile to ancient culture. They locked the

doors of the museum and even sold some of the statues inside.

The Belvedere was not the only collection of antique art. On 18 January 1471, in the Palazzo dei Conservatori on the Capitoline Hill, Pope Sixtus IV had opened to the public the first large collection of antiquities. There people were able to discover the *Spinario*

(or *Boy Picking a Thorn from his Foot*), probably of the 1st century BC, the archaic *She-Wolf*, and the *Lion Devouring a Horse*. Innocent VIII later had the colossal head of Constantine placed there.

These and other ancient statues aroused universal admiration. Princes and wealthy art lovers of Europe had copies made of them. Francesco Primaticcio (1504–70), an Italian painter and architect, was sent to Rome by King Francis I in 1540. He returned with more than a hundred cases of plaster casts and marbles he had bought. Philip II of Spain commissioned Diego Velázquez to draw all the statues of the Belvedere, with a view to adorning the royal palace in Madrid with imitations of them

The collecting fashion proves useful to archaeology

Encouraged by these early discoveries, Romans and foreigners began to excavate in earnest, seizing even the smallest fragment of marble.

In every palace, the courtyards and galleries became private museums; whole walls were encrusted with marble reliefs. One supremely

Rome contained no fewer than ninety private collections in the middle of the 16th century. Catalogues of the period, such as Ulisse Aldrovandi's *The Antiquities of the City of Rome*, 1576, enable us to understand how important collecting antique art had become, transforming palaces into museums. In the courtyard above, depicted by Maerten van Heemskerck, one sees an attempt to make use of modern architecture to display ancient statues.

Opposite: *Pope Leo X*, 1518, by Raphael (left). The *Apollo Belvedere* (centre) is a Roman copy of a Greek bronze of the 4th century BC by Leochares.

refined touch was to build one's house in the ruins.
Special envoys were sent to Rome from all over Europe to
find out about the discoveries and to make purchases;
columns, fragments of marble, and statues were thus
exported in vast quantities.

This passion of princes and of popes was undoubtedly
of great benefit to archaeology. In the 16th century
in the Baths of Caracalla (named for the 3rd-century
emperor), archaeologists for the Farnese family, leading
Roman aristocrats, unearthed some extraordinary
treasures: the famous *Hercules,* a colossal statue more than
3 m tall; the group of the *Bull*; a *Flora*; and a number of
mosaics.

The nobles of antiquity owned elaborately laid-out
gardens, and the excavation of these sites also produced a
large number of masterpieces. The *Hercules, Venus,
Asclepius,* and the busts of emperors from the gardens of
the Licinii were installed in Pope Julius III's country
palace, the Villa Giulia. In 1582 the pictorial group
known as the *Aldobrandini Marriage* (named after its
owners) was discovered on a wall in the gardens of the
Lamia family; this is one of the rare examples of large-
scale antique painting. In the gardens of the Sallusti, the
largest in antiquity, a colossal goddess' head, most
probably a Venus, was found. The statue's throne –
the 'Ludovisi Throne' – was not discovered until the
18th century.

In the course of these random excavations, in 1562 the
first fragments of the 'Forma Urbis', a marble map of
Rome made between AD 205 and 208, were unearthed.
The significance of this discovery was not grasped
immediately, but its publication in the next century
marked a decisive stage in Roman topography.

Thanks to the great construction projects, many new discoveries are made

During the building of the Via Leonina (now the Via di
Ripetta), large marble fragments of the mausoleum of
Augustus were discovered. This imperial tomb had been
built at the start of the empire. It was almost totally
destroyed in the 12th century and rebuilt and fortified
in the 13th century. Close by, in 1568, a part of the

The Forma Urbis
suffered much
damage from the 5th
century on. According
to a report by Flaminio
Vacca, the first fragments
of it were found in
May 1562; one is
shown on the right.

The mausoleum of
Augustus consisted
of a sort of drum, roughly
87 m in diameter, topped
by a cone of earth planted
with trees. Below,
an early 17th-century
view.

Mausoleum ab Augusto exstructum
Mausoleo di Augusto fatto per

e, posterisqz, eius sepuli Spectat ad Septemr" Pius-II-Papa Caput S·Andreæ in Basilica S·Petri transferendu solemniter curst Saghe
priä, et de sunt Guarda a Tramontana Pio·II·Papa fa portar la Testa di S·Andrea a S·Pietro solennemente .

Ara Pacis (Altar of Peace) was discovered. It had been begun in 13 BC and completed in 9 BC, during the golden age of Roman sculpture. The rest of the altar was not discovered until the 19th and 20th centuries.

One of the finest archaeological sites in Italy was Hadrian's Villa. The Emperor Hadrian (AD 76–138) had had a magnificent palace built very close to Tivoli, 25 km northeast of Rome. According to a 15th-century visitor, it was 'as large as a city', and every part of it bore the name of a famous site in the empire: there was the Lyceum, the Academy, the Canopus, the Pecile, and even the Underworld! In it, one could move from the libraries to the maritime theatre, from the gardens to the Temple of Serapis, from large baths to small ones. However, like Nero's Domus Aurea, the villa was abandoned after Hadrian's death and rapidly fell into a state of ruin.

Pirro Ligorio's map (opposite above) reveals the complexity of Hadrian's Villa. Its ruins are shown in this lithograph (above) and watercolour (opposite below).

Pirro Ligorio, topographer and antiquarian

Pirro Ligorio (c. 1500–83) was the first to explore the villa. An antiquarian, architect and topographer, he had been commissioned by Cardinal Ippolito d'Este to find the materials – marble and paving – and works of art for the building of a villa at Tivoli.

Rich mosaics of animals, such as this one of doves, were found in Hadrian's Villa.

This utilitarian commission did not prevent Ligorio from undertaking a serious excavation. He documented his work in the *Description of the Superb and Very Rich Villa of Hadrian.*

Ligorio was one of the finest archaeologists of the 16th century. Even though he did not hesitate to fabricate what he did not know, many of his intuitions have since

URBIS ROMAE SITVS CVM IIS QVAE
ADHVC CONSPICIVNTVR
VETER. MONVMET RELIQVIIS
PYRRHO LIGORIO NEAP. INVENT.
ROMAE · M · D · LXX.

AED · AVG ·

VIVARIVM

CASTRVM PRAE
TORIVM

Many maps of Rome were drawn in the middle of the 16th century. Pirro Ligorio's archaeological map (1551), reproduced here, takes the form of a kind of aerial view of the city as seen from the Janiculum, a fortified ridge to the west of Rome. One can make out the principal sites: the Palatine, the Forum, the Capitoline, and the ruins of the ancient monuments.

been proved correct. He personally visited all the sites in
Rome where excavations were in progress, and he left
reports and plans of his own work. His great talents as
an antiquarian, demonstrated by his *Dictionary of
Antiquities* and his archaeological map of Rome, led
Pope Pius IV to appoint him supervisor of the
monuments. In this position he left vivid testimony to
the contradictions of his age, divided as it was by an
impatience to resurrect the ancient city and a will to
modernize it. He proposed that the unearthed remains
should be left in place, but he was powerless in the face
of the destruction that went on. 'As the columns and
other parts were revealed,' he wrote of the Arch of
Augustus, 'I saw something that I could not have
imagined: most of the building's ornaments were sold
as though in a cattle market.... The inscriptions were lost
through ignorance and ill-will and...when I
cannot say any more about it, I weep.'

To modernize Rome, the popes condemn many ancient monuments

It was indeed an era of destruction, beginning
with a brief written on 17 December 1471 by
Pope Sixtus IV authorizing the architects of the
Vatican Library to undertake any excavation
they wished, with a view to obtaining stone.

Rome's leaders in the
16th century
wavered between the
protection of the ruins
and the modernization of
Rome. With Domenico
Fontana (1543–1607),
his official architect,
Sixtus V (above), pope
from 1585 to 1590,
conceived a construction
plan to open wide vistas,
to the detriment of the
ancient monuments.

Above left: the
building of the new
St Peter's, depicted in a
fresco by Giorgio Vasari
(1511–74).

Under Alexander VI (pope from 1492 to 1503) the Holy See put up for auction the Forum and the Colosseum, among other sites.

Apart from the excavations, it was the building of the new St Peter's that caused the greatest amount of destruction. On 22 July 1540 Pope Paul III condemned the Forum. Excavation permits, which had until then been issued jointly by the municipal authorities, the road inspectors and the Holy See, were granted exclusively and quite freely to the builders of the new basilica. In spite of protests, Pope Gregory XIII (1572–85) confirmed this measure and extended it to the

Domenico Fontana, in the frontispiece of his book on moving the Vatican obelisk.

This drawing shows St Peter's about 1536. It was completed in May 1590. Modern Rome was gradually being built.

sites of Ostia and Porto, two of Rome's ancient seaports. Finally, at the end of the century, Pope Sixtus V and his architect, Domenico Fontana, who was responsible for moving the obelisk from the Circus of Nero to its present position in front of St Peter's, had a number of celebrated remains demolished: a third of the Baths of Diocletian, part of the Claudian aqueduct, the Septizonium of Septimius Severus, and a large number of Early Christian or medieval buildings were destroyed, including the Patriarchum – the popes' former residence on the Lateran, which had been rich in oratories, chapels and mosaics – and the fine Oratory of Santa Croce, built in the 5th century by Pope Hilarius. The Oratory had

It took a hundred workers six days to lower the obelisk in the Circus of Nero, and a whole month to move it, with the help of enormous scaffolding and teams of men and animals. This contemporary depiction shows it scaffolded before the move. Beyond is old St Peter's, seen from the side, with new St Peter's rising on the left.

been adorned with a portico, fountains, marble basins, and magnificent golden mosaics.

Despite the destruction, the popes also strove to protect the monuments that were still intact – such as the columns of Trajan and Marcus Aurelius – and to limit the exporting of marble and the trade in antiquities.

On 20 August 1515 Raphael, the great painter from Urbino, was made commissioner of antiquities. He was responsible for prohibiting the destruction of inscriptions, a job in which he was not very successful, but his efforts did bring about a genuine improvement in the knowledge of the topography of Rome. The artist chose able collaborators: the epigrapher Jacopo Mazochio

Finally, on 10 September 1586, the obelisk was raised in St Peter's Square, in front of a silent crowd. More than 25 m high, the monolith was placed on an enormous pedestal and surrounded by four bronze lions.

and the antiquaries Fabio Calvo and Andrea Fulvio. The team's goal was to draw up an archaeological map of Rome 're-establishing its ancient form, its former perimeter, and the proportions of its different parts'. After Raphael's death in 1520 his friends continued his work. In 1521 Mazochio published a collection of inscriptions, and in 1527 Calvo published a map of Rome and Fulvio published his *Antiquities of Rome*.

A portrait of Charles V by a 16th-century painter.

"I pointed my musket in the direction of a denser and thicker skirmish and I took as my target a soldier who was right in the middle of it and whom I saw dominating others. Turning quickly to Alessandro and Cecchino, I ordered them to fire their muskets and showed them how to dodge the fire of those we were facing. When we had each fired two shots, I looked carefully over the wall and I noticed an extraordinary degree of confusion among the enemy: our fire had killed [the Connétable de] Bourbon."

Benvenuto Cellini

The sack of Rome interrupts the development of archaeology for twenty years

Shortly afterwards, on 6 May, troops of the Holy Roman Emperor Charles V occupied and ransacked the city. Fulvio and Calvo perished in the general massacre. This raid, one of the most destructive Rome ever suffered, marked an interruption in the history of archaeology. A strange silence reigned in the city at the end of 1527 after the raids and acts of sacrilege – a contemporary wrote that 'one no longer hears any bell, none of the churches is open, no masses are said any more.'

Studies of Roman topography were finally resumed twenty years later, with the work of Pirro Ligorio and with the discovery of the catacombs.

Unknown cities lie hidden beneath the suburbs of Rome

Fulvio had devoted books IV and V of his work to the Christian basilicas and cemeteries. Before him, Poggio Bracciolini, Cyriacus of Ancona and Maffeo Vegio (1407–58) had collected Christian inscriptions, but church history

1527.

BORBONE OCCISO, ROMANA IN MOENIA MILES
CAESAREVS RVIT, ET MISERANDAM DIRIPIT VRBEM.

There is no known contemporary representation of the sack of Rome. This depiction (left) was made later, adding scenes of violence and a few military details to a view of the city from the east.

Above: the death of the Connétable de Bourbon, in an engraving after Maerten van Heemskerk.

began in earnest only in the second half of the 16th
century, centering on the Oratory, where Giovanni
Borromeo, Onofrio Panvinio and Baronius studied Early
Christian funerary rites. Archaeological evidence was
painfully lacking. Nearly all the catacombs still lay
buried. In order to recover Early Christian
history, excavations had to be undertaken, and
a new methodology had to be invented.

On 31 May 1578, while work was being done in a
vineyard bordering on the Via Salaria, the ground
collapsed over an underground cemetery that
was decorated with paintings and Greek and
Latin inscriptions. It contained sarcophagi.
The preliminary exploration of this site,

The engravings on
these two pages
come from Antonio
Bosio's *Underground
Rome* (1632).

Nella Naue minore della Porta del Giuditt
nella base dell'ottaua colonna .

which attracted thousands of onlookers, was led by
the Spaniard Alfonso Ciacconio: he had the paintings
he found copied, but his exploration was limited.
It was not until several years later that a scholar,
Antonio Bosio, revealed the full implications of
this discovery.

Bosio, the 'inventor' of the catacombs

Bosio was only eighteen years old when he first
entered a catacomb in 1593 – the Catacombs of
Domitilla on the Via Ardeatina. Bosio and his friends
went bravely into the vast labyrinth in the depths of
the earth, attracted by the mystery and silence. The
sacred tunnels meandered off in every direction, and
the reflections of the candles on the walls made a deep
impression on the visitors. Suddenly they found
themselves in total darkness. Convinced that they
were going to die, they trembled at the idea of
desecrating those holy and inviolate places with their
dead bodies. They stumbled around for forty-eight
hours, until they found a way out. They promised
themselves that they would not undertake any further
expeditions of this kind without plenty of candles.

They illustrate Early
Christian funerary
rites in the catacombs.

This experience confirmed Bosio's dedication to his
vocation: from then on he devoted his time to the
exploration of the catacombs, reporting his findings in his
great book, *Underground Rome* (1632), a description of
all the catacombs and the paintings found in them.
The topographical order, the constant comparisons
made between the excavations, the texts and the
inscriptions – all reflect development in the field of
Christian archaeology. But Bosio was a man of the
16th century; he lacked a critical method. Nonetheless,
one can imagine the excitement aroused by his book
(not published until after his death) which presented a
picture of Rome as a sacred necropolis.

Bosio's work was used by Catholics and Protestants
alike in the dispute about whether the church was
faithful to the beliefs and practices of the Early
Christians. The discovery of the catacombs fuelled
a controversy which until that time had been based
only on texts.

Besides arousing the passion of archaeologists, the Roman ruins stimulated elegiac emotions and offered an ideal setting for genre paintings. In this view of the Forum one can barely make out the three columns of what was to be identified in the 19th century as the Temple of Vespasian on the right. The charming quality of this scene by Paul Bril (1554–1625) is due to the harmonious unity established between the ruins, nature, and human activities – a sort of contented nonchalance.

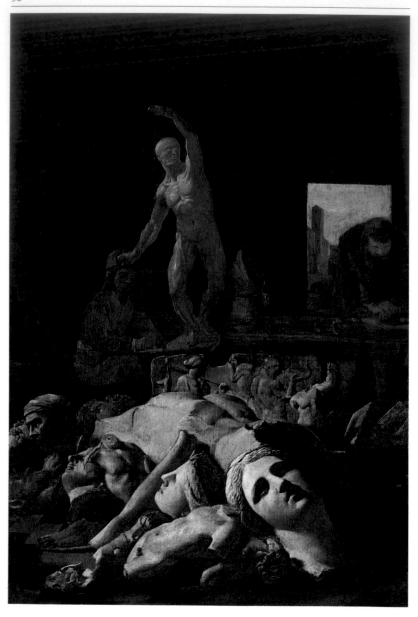

In the 18th century Rome and its remains were in everyone's heart – as a fad, as the favourite subject of artists, as an unforgettable goal of pilgrimage. The mania for antiquity raged throughout Europe. Wealthy collectors began to found museums, and the German archaeologist Johann Joachim Winckelmann laid the foundations of art history.

CHAPTER 3
FROM PRIVATE COLLECTIONS TO ART HISTORY

Remnants of Roman statuary were a popular subject with 18th-century painters. Opposite: *The Painter's Studio* by Michael Sweerts. Right: a painting by Ducros of the *Dioscuri* on the Capitol, greatly admired in the 18th century.

After Bosio, there was a lull in the progress of Christian archaeology: what people sought in the catacombs were relics and treasures. In the 17th and 18th centuries, scholars were busy publishing newly discovered inscriptions and commenting on ancient texts. Jean Mabillon (1632–1707), a Benedictine scholar, rediscovered the *Einsiedeln Itinerary*; Bernard de Montfaucon (1655–1741) published scholarly editions of the works of the church fathers and inventories of sources for Christian archaeology; Lodovico Antonio Muratori (1672–1750) published a commentary on the Papyri of Monza, which contained a list of the relics that were known at the time of

Gregory the Great (c. 540–604).

The archaeology of the pagan world continued on Renaissance lines. Great construction projects unearthed gold and silver coins, mosaics and reliefs; statues, including those of the Temple of Hadrian, were discovered. Papal edicts concerning the control of the excavations had as their main object the expansion of the popes' own collections. Clement XIV decided that discoveries would be divided among four beneficiaries: the pope, the Holy See, the owners of the land, and the people who had financed the projects.

Trade in antiquities becomes lucrative

Collecting and its natural corollary, trade, remained the primary motivating forces of the 'archaeologists': it was in order to sell antiquities or to copy them that Hadrian's Villa (1767) and the Appian Way (1771) were excavated. The restoration of masterpieces also became very lucrative, and scant attention was paid to questions of authenticity. For example, fragments of various statues were put together to form an Apollo, a Venus, or a Diana, depending on the demand. All the foreigners in Rome visited the studio of Bartolomeo Cavaceppi, the most gifted of all the Roman restorers, as if it were a museum.

Most of the buyers were British, as the fashion for the Grand Tour spread. Outstanding among the collectors were Thomas Coke of Holkham, William Weddell of Newby, and Charles Townley (whose marbles are now in the British Museum, London). Other Europeans, notably the French and Germans, were also influenced by the craze for antiquities. They became passionately interested in Rome and Italy. They bought copies and plaster casts of statues, which were cheaper and easier to export than originals.

Restorer Bartolomeo Cavaceppi (opposite above) perfected a new method of restoration that respected original styles, periods and materials; it was he who made restoration an art. *Charles Townley in his Gallery* by Johann Zoffany (above); *A Visit to the Dealer in Antiquities* by Jacques Sablet (opposite below).

"The English take everything out of Italy: paintings, statues.... Yet the English hardly ever take anything good."
Montesquieu (1689–1755)

Just as writers collected ancient texts, artists collected antique sculptures and paintings. Giorgio Vasari, the 16th-century historian of art, said of one engraver's house, 'it was full of so many objects that it was absolutely amazing.' These ancient and modern objects included marbles, bronzes and paintings. Antique art served not only as a model but as a source of prestige. By the 17th century this was confirmed: popes and princes were competing to own the most magnificent collections. This painting, *The Collection of Cornelis van der Geest,* is by Willem van Haecht.

Goethe once proposed that a museum be created in Rome in which plaster casts of all the antiquities that had been discovered could be displayed.

The great collectors

Renaissance palaces were decorated with antique fragments; in the 18th century, buildings were put up specifically to house gigantic collections. Cardinal Alessandro Albani, a nephew of Pope Clement XI, had the first villa-museum built on the Via Salaria. There he positioned obelisks, columns, sarcophagi, statues and imperial busts amid bushes, trees and fountains; reliefs were recessed into the walls of the inner rooms. Daedalus and Icarus, Apollo and Diana, Orpheus and Eurydice took up residence. After its completion in 1763 by the architect Carlo Marchionni, the Villa Albani was said to be a truly fairy-tale residence.

For a Borghese prince, the Villa Pinciana was transformed into a museum of antiquities, and false ruins were created in the immense gardens – a stadium,

The entrance to the underground ruins of Otricoli (opposite above).

The gardens of the Villa Borghese (opposite below) were laid out to display statues and ruins. The Casino (below) was built between 1613 and 1615 and later enlarged; here the Asprucci family kept 'the queen of private collections'. The grounds now comprise the largest public park in Rome, and the Casino is one of its finest museums.

a Temple of Diana,
and a Temple of Asclepius.

Nothing is too beautiful for the Pio-Clementino Museum

Founded by Pope Clement XIV
(1767–74) and completed by Pius
VI (1775–99), the Pio-Clementino
Museum in the Vatican was opened
to the public only once a year.
Pius VI was not worried about the
cost: he bought from dealers and
collectors or simply appropriated
statues from many buildings,
taking the bust of
Hadrian and a
Minerva from the
Castel Sant'
Angelo and the

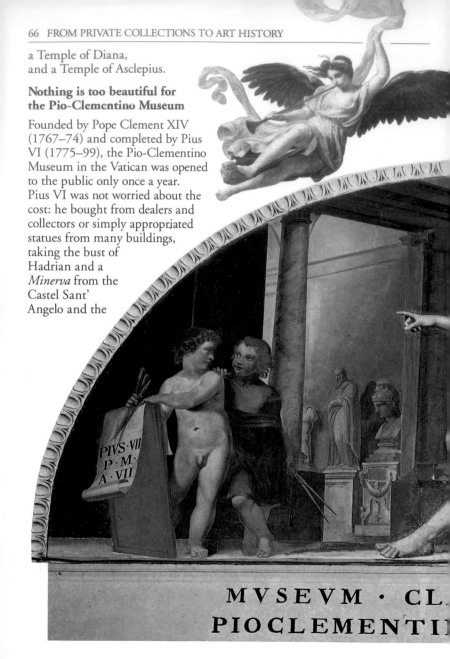

PIVS·VII
P·M·
A·VII

MVSEVM · CL

PIOCLEMENTI

sarcophagus of St Helena from the Lateran. He gave himself preemptive rights over all the discoveries and amassed more than three hundred marbles in the course of his pontificate. He surrounded himself with talented agents and advisers who catalogued the collection in seven scholarly tomes, confirming the supreme reputation of the Vatican holdings.

The pope organized excavations, especially in Latium, the region surrounding Rome. At Castrum Novum, a former Roman colony,

Founded by Clement XIV and Pius VI, the Pio-Clementino Museum was enlarged under Pius VII (1800–23) by the creation of the Chiaramonti Museum, of which this fresco is an allegorical representation.

AMONTANVM
· ADIECTVM

fragments of statues, inscriptions, and gold coins from the reign of Nero were discovered. In Salona, also formerly a colony of Rome, they found the *Crouching Venus,* which is now in the Vatican. At Otricoli, 75 km north of Rome, an ancient town was almost totally uncovered (including a basilica, theatre, and baths) and its plan drawn up.

The present entrance to the Tomb of the Scipios (left) opens off the most famous Roman road, the Appian Way. In former times the building (shown in an etching by Giovanni Battista Piranesi, opposite above) faced northwest. Only a small part of it remains today.

The funerary rites of the ancient Romans become clearer with the discovery of the Tomb of the Scipios

In May 1780 several underground chambers containing sarcophagi were discovered outside the Porta San Sebastiano in Rome. The tomb belonged to the Scipios, a great Roman family that was most famous for having triumphed over the Carthaginians and their leader, Hannibal, in the 3rd century BC.

Visitors were immediately attracted by the tomb's oldest sarcophagus, that of Barbatus, who conquered the Etruscans in 298 BC. Barbatus' merits are praised in his epitaph: 'Lucius Cornelius Scipio Barbatus, the son of Gnaeus, a courageous and wise man; he was a consul, censor, and councillor in your country. He conquered Taurasia and Cisauna, in the Samnium, and subjugated the whole of Lucania, whence he brought back hostages.'

When the labyrinth of the tomb was fully explored, it yielded a dozen more sarcophagi, dating between the 3rd century BC and the 1st century AD. Pius VI had the sarcophagus of Barbatus and the inscriptions transported to the Pio-Clementino Museum; the other sarcophagi were smashed, the funerary objects were sold, and the bones that were found were dispersed.

On the Appian Way, outside the Porta San Sebastiano, the Tomb of the Household of Augustus (left below) was a vast structure made up of three adjacent halls containing a thousand niches for urns. Bianchini's view conveys the sense of grandeur felt by those who discovered this tomb. In the 19th century other vaults with recesses for funerary urns – known as 'columbaria', dovecotes, from the resemblance between the two types of structure – were discovered along the Appian Way, especially in this area.

In the 17th century it was still believed that, until late in the empire, cremation was the only way Romans had disposed of their dead. This thesis seemed to have been supported in 1777 by the discovery of the *ustrinum* of Augustus, the sacred precinct where the bodies of the emperor and his family and those of his first successors had been burned. But the discovery of the Tomb of the Scipios three years later showed that, from an early date, Romans had also buried their dead.

Further discoveries subsequently confirmed the coexistence of the two practices; sometimes there were both urns of ashes and sarcophagi within a single tomb.

The Palace of Domitian

In ancient times the Palatine Hill was reserved for the palaces of the emperors. It had become covered with

The idea of creating gardens on the Palatine Hill occurred to Paul III Farnese during the building of the triumphal way in the Forum for the Emperor Charles V in 1536. The choice of this hill, where the palaces of the Roman emperors stood, was largely political: it made the pope appear as the true ruler of Rome and its genuine patron. This drawing was made in 1759 by Charles Natoire.

vines and pasture in the Middle Ages, and by the 16th century only a few ruins were still visible. In 1535 Pope Paul III Farnese had purchased part of the land and built a splendid villa and garden over the ancient structures, the remains of which survive today. When the Farnese family died out in the late 17th century, the dukes of Parma grew bergamot, vines and artichokes there, while feverishly searching for treasures. In 1720 Francis I, duke of Parma, organized a systematic excavation of the site. He entrusted the responsibility of drawing up the inventories to Francesco Bianchini, who was commissioner of antiquities at the time.

Work was confined to the southeastern slope of the hill, that is, to a part of the former Palace of the Flavians, built between AD 82 and 96 by the Emperor Domitian. The excavators uncovered three splendid rooms: the basilica, with its hemispherical vault; the throne room, with its sixteen fluted marble columns and twelve niches that held twelve colossal statues of black basalt; and

The Temple of Saturn (above) encrusted with houses in the 18th century.

The coin below, from the time of Septimius Severus, shows a building in the form of a circus; it is the Stadium of Domitian (built at the end of the 1st century AD), the present Piazza Navona.

finally the 'lararium'. In this room they found a cone-shaped dark stone about 1 m high. It has since disappeared. None of the scholars of the time knew what it was. It may have been the Black Stone, a symbol of the goddess Cybele, which was transported to Rome at the end of the 3rd century BC to ward off the Carthaginian threat.

This palace was sumptuous, and it was ransacked rather than excavated: the two fluted columns of *giallo antico* marble that stood on either side of the door were dispersed; the cornices and sculptures disappeared. The duke of Parma kept two statues of Hercules, a Bacchus, a head of Zeus, and the reliefs for himself. Damage was done to the magnificent frescoes that were found beneath the palace in two rooms dating from an even earlier period: the House of the Griffins, named for the stucco griffins that formed its decor, and the Aula of Isis, a 1st-century room containing paintings of Egyptian subjects.

The Palatine Hill (left) was the centre of intense archaeological activity in the 18th century before it became a place for romantic walks.

Looking toward the Arch of Constantine along the eastern slope of the Palatine, crowned by the great apsed structure of the Temple of Venus and Rome (left below). The largest of the triumphal arches of Rome stands on the road that leads from the Circus Maximus to the Arch of Titus. It was built by Constantine after his victory at the Milvian Bridge in AD 312 to commemorate his mystical vision of the Cross during the battle. For a long time it was difficult to date the arch because of the presence of architectural elements and sculptures of different periods; Constantine had appropriated and re-used many different fragments.

Piranesi's grandiose reconstruction of the area around the circular Mausoleum of Hadrian beside the Tiber, from his book on the Campus Martius.

While Domitian's Palace revealed the baroque nature of Flavian art, these paintings executed earlier in the 1st century AD revealed a more classical style, which would also be found at Pompeii.

The ruins depicted

As archaeology became more serious, inventories of the sites, maps, and architectural drawings flourished. They

In Piranesi's time, the Forum, then known as the Campo Vaccino, was a field in which fragments of the still-buried ancient ruins were visible (left).

were stimulated by the enthusiasm of publishers and booksellers. It was in the prints of the Venetian Giovanni Battista Piranesi (1720–78) that the artists' concern for the picturesque and the scholars' concern for investigation and accuracy were reconciled. His work brings together all the themes of the period: *Views of Rome* (1748–78); *Roman Antiquities* (1756), etchings of antique remains; and the *Carceri* (*Prisons*) of 1745, a kind of fantasy architecture.

Reliquiae Pontis Triumphalis seu Vaticani
Vide indicem ruinar. num. 36.

Born in Venice in 1720, Piranesi (in profile, above) first studied architecture and then engraving. He moved to Rome around 1740 and stayed there until his death in 1778; in Rome he drew inspiration from the ruins.

The ravages of time

The Colosseum was ravaged and used for many purposes: Sixtus V thought of transforming it into a woollen mill, and others turned it into a place of devotion – séances were even held there. It was seriously damaged by an earthquake in 1703; Pope Clement XI (1700–21) had the arches filled in with wooden fences, which are visible in this painting by Canaletto (1697–1768).

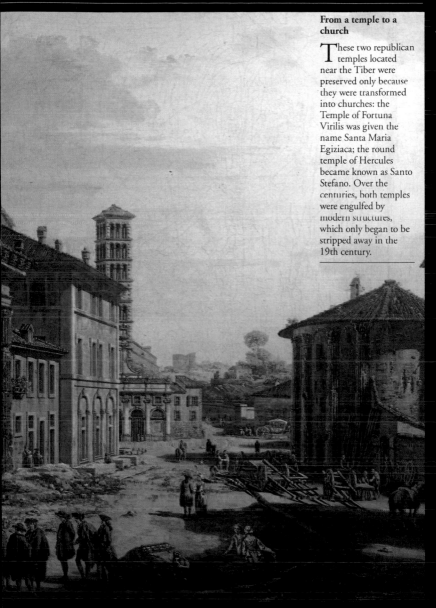

From a temple to a church

These two republican temples located near the Tiber were preserved only because they were transformed into churches: the Temple of Fortuna Virilis was given the name Santa Maria Egiziaca; the round temple of Hercules became known as Santo Stefano. Over the centuries, both temples were engulfed by modern structures, which only began to be stripped away in the 19th century.

Fragments of antiquities

This *Gallery of Ancient Rome* was painted in 1757 by Giovanni Paolo Pannini (1691–1765). One finds in this painting most of the great themes of the time: the popularity of *vedute* (views of monuments), of antique decoration, of collecting fragments of antique objects, and a sense of playfulness. The game is to identify the objects: on the left, the *Farnese Hercules* and the *Dying Gaul*; on the right, the *Spinario* or *Thorn-Puller* and the *Laocoön*. Among the monuments, we glimpse on the left the three columns of the Temple of Vespasian, the Arch of Constantine, and the interior of the Pantheon; on the right, the Colosseum. The meticulous precision of these depictions reflects the increasingly meticulous studies of the archaeologists.

Piranesi's maps of Rome, like the works of so many of his predecessors in the 16th and 17th centuries, reflect a genuine passion for remains and fragments. His map of the Campus Martius looks like the ancient marble map of Rome, the Forma Urbis, but Piranesi conveys his own idea of the magnificence of Rome rather than faithfully reconstructing the site itself. In contrast, his map of Hadrian's Villa is of undeniable scholarly value.

New beginnings: the birth of the history of art

Piranesi envisioned a monumental and inventive Roman art, which he defended against the ideas of expert proponents of Greek art as the ultimate expression of antiquity. The quarrel between the champions of Greece and those of Rome was what finally brought archaeology into the modern era.

For the Prussian scholar Johann Joachim Winckelmann (1717–68), who had been living in Rome since 1755, Greek art alone had risen to the level of ideal beauty. Thus 'the only means by which we may attain greatness,' he argued, 'and – if such were possible – be inimitable, is to imitate the ancients.'

Starting with this theory, which was one of the main tenets of the Neo-Classical movement that became fashionable all over Europe, Winckelmann laid the foundations of the first history of art. He described four periods: the Ancient (Archaic Greece), the Sublime (5th century BC), the Beautiful (4th century BC), and the Decadent (2nd and 1st centuries BC and the Roman period).

In this system Rome had little prestige, but the classification did at least make a truly historical approach to the subject possible. Antiquarians and popes had always neglected considerations of history,

For Winckelmann, the 'noble simplicity and tranquil grandeur' of Greek art were confirmed by the pure whiteness of the statues. Below: the *Capitoline Amazon*, a Roman copy of a Greek original by Polykleitos.

HISTOIRE
DE
L'ART
CHEZ LES ANCIENS.
Par Mr. J. WINCKELMANN,

*Préſident des Antiquités à Rome, Membre de la
Société Royale des Antiquités de Londres,
de l'Académie de Peinture de St. Luc à
Rome, & de l'Académie Etruſque
de Cortone, &c.*

OUVRAGE TRADUIT DE L'ALLEMAND. *par
hub*

TOME PREMIER.

A AMSTERDAM,
Chez E. VAN HARREVELT,

motivated as they were to accumulate artifacts or to maintain social prestige. Because of Winckelmann, restoration was subjected to strict rules requiring a preliminary study of the styles and precise dating. Thus Winckelmann made ancient art, which had until then only been coveted or imitated, into a subject of historical scholarship, and he made the history of art into one of the main branches of archaeology. His *History of Ancient Art* (1764) was widely circulated and translated into several European languages.

It is an irony of history that Winckelmann, scholarly theorist and passionate champion of Greek art, did not know that a large proportion of the statues he had admired as Greek were, in fact, Roman copies. His beloved Apollo Belvedere was a marble replica of a lost bronze original made in Athens some four hundred years earlier, around 330 BC. Yet he founded an entire school, and the discovery of the originals in Greece and Asia Minor was viewed by Winckelmann's disciples as corroborating his new theories.

Born in 1717, the son of a cobbler, Winckelmann (above left) studied theology and the humanities. His passions for mythology and ancient art led him to Rome. He visited the excavations of Herculaneum, Pompeii and Paestum, and became a friend of Cardinal Albani, who employed him as a librarian. He was assassinated by an unidentified person in 1768.

"The pope will deliver to the French Republic a hundred paintings, busts, vases, and statues chosen by the envoys who will be sent to Rome; these items will include the bronze bust of Junius Brutus and the marble bust of Marcus Brutus, both of which are on the Capitol, as well as five hundred manuscripts..."

Article 8 of the Armistice of Bologna

CHAPTER 4
ROME UNDER NAPOLEON

Napoleon's administration showed a constant interest in the Colosseum, clearing and restoring it as well as conducting excavations – shown in this painting by Hubert Robert (opposite) – which yielded many fragments of marble and coins. An 1830 diagram of the Colosseum (right).

The French in Rome, and the last great collection of Roman art

The French occupation of Rome in the 1790s led to extensive pillaging, which was made legal by the Armistice of Bologna signed by Pope Pius VI and Napoleon Bonaparte. It was confirmed by the Treaty of Tolentino in 1797. As they did in other Italian cities, the French sequestered the great private fortunes, including the rich collections of the Vatican.

Napoleon was in Egypt on 28 July 1799 when the long convoy of the spoils of Rome arrived in Paris in richly ornamented wagons. Canvases by Raphael and Titian, antique manuscripts and sculptures – the *Apollo Belvedere, Laocoön* and *Spinario* – and many other marvels made up the collection of antiquities of the French Museum of the Republic. This museum was later renamed the Central Museum of the Arts and was ultimately installed in the Louvre.

Planning and setting up the museum took two years. It opened in November 1801, when 117 works went on display. This was the last great collection made up entirely of Roman art; after the discoveries of the 18th and 19th centuries, objects of more diverse origins were brought together in museums, as in the British

The fresco below by Francesco Hayez evokes the return to Rome of the treasures plundered a few years earlier by the French troops (shown in the engraving above). In the fresco's foreground is a personification of the Tiber River surrounded by *putti* who are looking towards Monte Mario at the arrival of the procession. On the left is a portrait of the English official W. R. Hamilton (1777–1859), who played an important role in the recovery of Rome's heritage.

Museum, which held the largest collection of Greek art at the time.

The Treaty of Vienna in 1815 brought about the end of Napoleon's museum, since it included very strict clauses on the subject of restitution. Thanks to the intervention of the Italian sculptor Antonio Canova (1757–1822), the pope recovered almost all his property. Some works were bought by the French, including a large part of the Borghese collection, which formed the core of the Musée Royal, later called the Louvre.

Pius VII and the legal protection of the Italian artistic heritage

There had been some strong reactions in France to Napoleon's pillaging of Rome. In his *Letters to Miranda*, published during Napoleon's Italian campaign, Quatremère de Quincy, a French architect with a passion for archaeology, recognized the need to safeguard the

Archaeologist Ennio Quirino Visconti.

A series of frescoes by different painters commissioned by Antonio Canova was to illustrate the stages of the restoration of the Italian artistic heritage and the installation of the new collections in the Chiaramonti Museum.

artistic heritage of Italy. He pointed out how damaging it
would be for the works of art to be moved and
formulated for the first time the idea that there was an
essential relationship between an object and its place of
origin.

When Pius VII was elected pope in 1800, he, too,
was preoccupied by the question of that heritage. By
an edict written in 1802, he banned excavation and
export of art objects without papal authorization,
obliged individuals to draw up annual inventories
of their collections, and granted a budget for the
expansion of the museums and the improvement of
the teaching of archaeology.

By taking these steps, which were confirmed in
1820 by the Edict of Pacca, Pius VII established the
first state protection of artistic heritage, foreshadowing

Architect Quatremère
de Quincy (above).
Slaves clearing the ruins,
1830 (below).

the gradual disappearance of private collections during the 19th century.

Two men were appointed to implement these decisions: the sculptor Antonio Canova, supervisor of the artistic treasures, was entrusted with the task of inspecting and expanding the museums; Carlo Fea, commissioner of antiquities, was given the role of overseeing the ancient monuments and the churches. Their jurisdiction extended to all of the Papal States, and they were to exert their influence on art and archaeology for more than twenty years.

The clearing of the Forum mobilizes the archaeologists

Directed by Carlo Fea, excavations were resumed, principally in the Roman Forum. At the beginning of the 19th century, this was a field crossed by two rows of elm trees and surrounded by isolated houses and stonecutters' shops. Cattle grazed around the half-buried ruins; a huge basin that had been placed near the Temple of Castor and Pollux in 1565 was being used as a water trough.

The archaeologists' main task was to uncover the ruins in order to find the original level of the ground. Then they were to protect the ruins by fencing them off. These measures were applied first to the arches of Constantine and Septimius Severus. One important innovation was that prisoners and slaves took part in these excavations. There were more than a hundred of them at work on the Colosseum; they had cannonballs chained to their feet and were guarded by soldiers.

Yet Pius VII could not afford to begin a genuine programme of restoration. The few projects that had been started at the beginning of his pontificate soon slowed down or were suspended as Rome fell into decay and people began to move away from the city. In the

This view of the Forum from the Capitol shows the state of the excavations at the beginning of the 19th century and gives special prominence to the Arch of Septimius Severus, which was uncovered and surrounded by a fence. In the centre of the painting, one can see the Column of Phocas and, on the right, the columns of the Temple of Saturn.

opinion of the first secretary of the French Embassy, Rome was on the verge of collapse: 'Sitting in the same dust, pagan Rome was sinking into its tombs', he said, 'and Christian Rome was gradually going back down into its catacombs.'

The great excavations set the pace of life in Rome

After it became a 'free and imperial city', in 1809, and then a department of the French Empire in August of the same year, Rome, declared by Napoleon to be the second capital of the empire, received large subsidies. At the same time, archaeology was rapidly being transformed. Before, excavations had been conducted sporadically – undertaken for treasure and readily abandoned.

But from this time on, digging was no longer done simply in order to exploit a ruin but to uncover it according to the methods tested by Pius VII. To an even greater extent, restoring huge sites such as Pompeii and analysing their architectural structures became a goal.

The French undertook large-scale excavations in Rome. These archaeologists were the first to tackle a problem that urban planners have still not resolved: in what way could ruins be allowed to remain a part of the fabric of a modern city? It was said that two cities had to be distinguished: one would have to be modernized and the unnecessary monuments demolished, including some of the churches – there were thought to be too many – and the other would have to be restored by means of extensive excavations.

Archaeology becomes official and institutionalized

The French government began by creating various institutions. The

This portrait of Pope Pius VII (above) is by Jacques-Louis David.

The clearing of the Temple of Vespasian, known at the time as the Temple of Jupiter Tonans (the Thunderer), was one of the most spectacular achievements of the French administration of Rome. Above left: the scaffolding needed in clearing the architrave. Left: in these views and plans (insets) one sees (far left) the capitals of three columns jutting out from the earth and (near left) the columns and the Tabularium – the large Roman building on the right – that reappeared after the earth was cleared away.

Commission for Antique Monuments and Civic Buildings, founded in 1810 and replaced by the Commission for the Embellishment of Rome in 1811, conferred the principal role on the prefect of Rome: he would issue the permits for excavations, decide the pace of the projects, and determine the fate of the objects uncovered.

The teaching of archaeology was also reorganized. Filippo Aurelio Visconti proposed dividing the subject into three parts: mythology, the history of art, and archaeology itself. This third part would be useful to both artists and historians. Its object, Visconti said, was 'in theory and in practice, to order, interpret, understand, distinguish, and appreciate antique works, that is, their period, their value, and what they represent and signify.' Of all the measures taken, this was the most original.

Count Pierre Antoine Daru (1767–1829) was Napoleon's representative in Rome.

In this run-down city the French had also found an impoverished and unemployed population. They decided to employ the poor on the excavations. Formed into contingents of a hundred people (men, women and

L eft: the Basilica of Constantine. Stendhal noted in 1828: 'The three large arches that we saw occupied the whole length of the nave to the right of the entrance.... The vault was supported by eight thick columns.... The excavations ordered by Napoleon led to the discovery of the floor of this monument; it is made up of purple and cipollino marble.'

children), there were four hundred, and later two thousand, working for the administration.

De Tournon wrote in his *Statistical Studies on Rome* in 1831: 'It was thanks to those excavations that an enthusiasm for work spread among the men whose youth had been spent in poverty and indifference toward the future. Initially, there was a scarcity of labourers who were willing to perform what were considered to be the heaviest tasks; but later there

was not enough work to employ all those who sought work, such had been the influence of the examples that had been set and so rapid had been the industrial education of the people!'

An exemplary excavation: the Forum of Trajan

The column that the Emperor Trajan had erected in AD 113 to commemorate his victory over the Dacians had survived through the centuries without changing its name or suffering any real damage. The statue of the emperor that had once surmounted it, however, had been replaced

T he Domus Aurea of Nero was built over by the Baths of Trajan. Its buried rooms had been discovered shortly after 1500; the French organized further excavations. Opposite: a view in 1817. Above: a plan of 1811, showing the complex remains of the villa running diagonally across the outline of the Baths. (The site was misidentified as the Baths of Titus.)

by a statue of St Peter at the end of the 16th century.
Rubble had accumulated near the column, and it was
surrounded by more recent buildings.

Pius VI had had its base cleared down to the ancient
paving stones so that it stood in a kind of ditch, bordered
to the south by the convents of St Euphemia and the
Holy Ghost, to the west by a number of buildings, and
to the north by two churches. The plan of 1810 was
to widen the square, to lower it all to a uniform level, and
then to excavate it. The demolition of the buildings and
of the two convents was begun in March 1812 and
completed in December of that year. Excavations began
the following May.

The first results were not very encouraging: a few
broken columns, a vase, a head. A year later, the finds
included various statues, an empress' head, and a
fragment of a colossal statue made of porphyry   a
purplish-red stone associated with emperors.

The most important building to be uncovered was the
central section of the ancient Basilica Ulpia, but several
pieces of the portico of the libraries were found as well.
Bases of twenty columns and the remains of marble
paving of the basilica were revealed. The space cleared in
this way was a vast shallow pit surrounded by a wall.

Work continued on the square through the 19th and
into the first years of the 20th century. It was followed
by large-scale clearance projects organized by Benito
Mussolini in the 1930s.

The 'Garden of the Capitol', an over-ambitious project

Near Trajan's Forum, the most ancient district of
Rome was desolate and dilapidated. The arena of the
Colosseum was completely covered with soil and
rubble; part of the facade had collapsed, and another
part was held up by a kind of spur that had been built
in 1803. The work done under Pius VII had not really
changed the appearance of the Forum. And as for the
two temples near the Tiber, they appeared to be sinking
into the ground.

In order to provide a fitting setting for this group
of monuments, plans were made to create a huge

Napoleon had the
Vendôme Column
(above) erected in Paris,
modelling it on Trajan's
Column (opposite).

After the Napoleonic
excavations in 1820
Pope Pius VII had
Trajan's Forum
surrounded by a wall
(opposite below).

Left: The Temple of Saturn, filled with houses. Visible far left are the three half-buried columns of the Temple of Jupiter Tonans or Vespasian.

Left below: Giuseppe Valadier, an architect who assisted with the excavation of Trajan's Forum and other projects.

archaeological promenade, the 'Garden of the Capitol'. It was supposed to include the Capitol, the Forum, and the Colosseum. This project, which eventually proved to be too costly and unwieldy and was never completed, involved the demolition of the modern buildings (which, needless to say, would have aroused the hostility of the inhabitants), the uncovering of the monuments, and, most important, the levelling of the ground over a vast area. In spite of these obstacles work began in 1810: six hundred workers were employed in the Forum.

They began by clearing the Temple of Concord, the Temple of Antoninus and Faustina, and the Basilica of Constantine, the floor of which was covered with so much earth that the vaults barely appeared above the ground. A year later the three bays had been exposed down to pavement level. Near the Arch of Titus, the convent of Santa Francesca Romana, which abutted the arch, was demolished, as was the church that had been built over part of the ruins of the Temple of Venus and Rome. The bases of both of the ancient buildings were uncovered in the last stage of the project. Further work exposed the Temples of Jupiter Tonans and Saturn and the Arch of Septimius Severus.

The Temple of Antoninus and Faustina (left) was built in AD 141 by Antoninus Pius in honour of his wife, Faustina; it was dedicated to the emperor on his death in 161. The temple is one of the best-preserved monuments of Rome and of the Forum. A young French architect, J.-F. Ménager, led an excavation which uncovered the bases of the columns and the stairs up to the building and drew an idealized reconstruction of it (below).

Architects assisting archaeology

The architect Giuseppe Valadier was involved in almost every project for the modernization of Rome, such as the redesigning of the space around the Pantheon; but he and other architects also participated actively in the

Ménager's drawing includes many errors; the portrayal of the apotheosis of Antoninus and Faustina on the pediment, for example, is completely imaginary. Above: a detail showing a capital.

archaeological work and decisively altered the conception of what an excavation really entailed. They demanded the comprehensive clearing of the substructures of a building and the analysis of architectural groups as entities, to enable the complete topography of a site to be reconstructed. This was the approach followed by Carlo Fea, who tried to rediscover the structure of the Forum and planned a vast excavation of Ostia, Rome's ancient port to the west on the Tiber.

Such, also, was the vision of Giuseppi Guattani, a member of the Commission for the Embellishment of Rome and an associate on the project of the restoration of the Forum. In his *Guide to Rome,* he advised visitors to climb to the top of Trajan's Column to understand the layout of the city. He suggested the use of a schematic map of the monuments so that the dynamics of their interrelationships could be grasped. The guides produced in the 19th century were no longer merely descriptions of the city; recent topographical analyses and assessments of the archaeological discoveries had shed light on the structural organization of the sites, and thereby all of Rome.

A time of assessments

The projects of this period were undoubtedly overly ambitious. The French occupation, which was at first, in the words of the French writer François-Auguste-René de Chateaubriand, 'despicable and despoiling', and later

In addition to the projects he organized to restore the ancient monuments, Napoleon wanted to improve the modern city, for instance by enlarging the square in front of the Pantheon and creating a promenade to the north of Rome. Most of his projects remained on the drawing board, but the northern area of the Piazza del Popolo, notably the Pincio (left), was transformed in accordance with the terms of Article 7 of Napoleon's decree of 27 July 1811: 'The plans that have been submitted to us for the promenade near the Square of the People are hereby approved. To this effect, the convent of the People and its dependencies shall be demolished; this promenade shall be called the Garden of the Great Caesar.'

merely 'iniquitous', aroused an almost universal hostility – and yet archaeology benefited from it enormously. The French novelist Stendhal, always quick to be critical, here found something to praise: 'Thanks to the immense projects that have been undertaken, the appearance of the ancient monuments has changed completely since 1809, and the scholarship that concerns itself with them has become more reasonable.'

Major scholarly excavations took place in the Forum, on the Appian Way, and in the catacombs during the 19th century. This was also a time of classification and ordering of materials – texts, inscriptions and objects – that had been accumulated since the Renaissance in a sometimes disordered and hasty manner.

CHAPTER 5
THE AGE OF REASON

In May 1864 crowds assembled at the Palace of Cardinal Righetti, located over the ruins of Pompey's Theatre, in order to witness the raising of a gilded bronze *Hercules* 3.82 m tall (opposite).

The equestrian statue of Marcus Aurelius (right).

In 1863, nearing the 2600th anniversary of the founding of Rome, an item of news was stirring scholarly circles: an exceptionally important statue had just been discovered at the Prima Porta, one of the city gates. Scholars had known for a long time that Livia Drusilla, the wife of the Emperor Augustus, had had a magnificent villa built for herself to the north of Rome. A certain Giuseppe Gagliardi had identified the site. On 20 April, below ground level, near a large room decorated with blue and green landscapes, he discovered a statue of Augustus in perfect condition. Pope Pius IX immediately claimed the masterpiece: it would fit so well in the Chiaramonti Museum!

In the *Augustus of Prima Porta,* the emperor projects a serene majesty. The universe is engraved upon his breastplate: a bearded old man at the top represents the sky; to the left is the Chariot of the Sun, accompanied by the winged Dawn and the spirit of Sunrise; on the lower part are the Earth, Apollo, and Artemis.

Amateurs' luck

Amateurs such as Gagliardi had no difficulty obtaining permission from the Holy See to carry out their own excavations in exchange for a share of the discoveries. It was an amateur who found the paving stones of the ancient Via Latina to the south of Rome, and on each side of it, a number of tombs that were rich in paintings, stuccos, and funerary objects, some of which were sold and dispersed. South of the Aventine lay Emporium, built in the 2nd century BC as the port of Rome. Here another amateur, Pietro Ercole Visconti, discovered one of the great stores of marble of antiquity – a large number of blocks of alabaster, onyx and serpentine in the antique colours of yellow, green and red. Pius IX distributed these materials to churches all over the world and showered the lucky explorer with his favours, including making him a baron.

Thus, the history of archaeology still included such chance discoveries – sensational news that attracted illustrious visitors as well as pillaging and scandal. In the 1860s everyone heard about the trial of the Marchese Giovanni Campana, a collector who was banished from Rome for extorting

considerable sums of money from the state pawnbrokers.
But this was also a time of major, systematic excavations
led by such archaeologists as Nibby,
Canina and De' Rossi, whose research
was objective and whose method was
more scientific.

Nibby, Fea: quarrels in the Forum

In 1827 Antonio Nibby was
appointed director of the excavations
in the Forum. He cleared the
northern part of it, the Tabularium,
the Temple of Concord, and the
Temple of Venus
and Rome. In the
course of his work,
however, he arrived
at conclusions
that put him at
loggerheads
with Carlo Fea,
the former
commissioner of antiquities, and most other
archaeologists.

Fenced off, full of trees
and birds, the garden
painted on a wall in the
House of Livia (top) has a
charm and an air of
mystery that are unique
in Roman painting.

The Tomb of
Pomponius Hylas
was discovered in 1831.
The main hall of the
columbarium (above) was
decorated with stuccos
and paintings.

At the foot of the Capitoline Hill near the Temple of
Saturn stood three columns. Their entablature bore a
fragment of an inscription – ESTITVER – that led
scholars to believe the columns to be the remains of the

DU·TEMPLE·
DE·LA·PAIX

Temple of Jupiter Tonans (the Thunderer). Nibby relied on recent discoveries and old texts to reveal the truth: in the *Einsiedeln Itinerary*, the medieval guide to Rome, he found the entire inscription, proving that in fact these columns were the remains of the Temple of Vespasian. This temple was built in honour of the emperor, who ruled from AD 69 to 79, and was completed on the death of his son, Titus. The emperors Septimius Severus and Caracalla had it restored – [R]ESTITVER[VNT] – over a century later.

In the same way, the archaeologist identified 'the three very high brick vaults' that stand on the left of the Forum as one looks towards the Colosseum. In the Middle Ages this huge building was thought to be the Temple of Romulus. It had been referred to as the Temple of Peace since the 15th century. But in Nibby's view it could only be the Basilica of Constantine, which had been built at the beginning of the 4th century.

At the same time, in spite of Fea's protests, Nibby identified the true Temple of Peace, an impressive architectural group where the Emperor Vespasian had assembled 'all that men were curious about' – gold vases

Stendhal liked to poke fun at Antonio Nibby (above), who renamed the monuments. And yet, without even crediting him, Stendhal 'borrowed' whole pages of Nibby's *Roman Itinerary* in his own writing.

from Judea, statues, and a rich library. The famous Forma Urbis was placed there in the 3rd century AD.

Discourse on method

These scholarly disputes did not escape the irony of the satirists; yet methods of analysis had progressed. In the 16th century dogmatism and falsification had been the standard weapons of the scholars who, like artists,

sought a model in Rome: 'What I established on the Forum', declared Bartolomeo Marliano, 'is the absolute truth; and if old Romulus himself had risen from his tomb to tell me that he had built his forum differently, I would answer him thus: "Oh Romulus! You have crossed the River Lethe, and because of that you have forgotten the location of your city to such an extent that you do not know what you are saying!"' The 19th century saw the triumph of the philological spirit. The critical method applied to texts was also applied to the works of art and monuments, which scholars attempted to identify, date, and locate.

Historical analysis of the findings was not attempted until the end of the 19th century. By about 1850 the excavation of the Forum had almost been completed. Its structure was now better understood, thanks to Nibby's

Opposite: this 1814 drawing of the 'Temple of Peace', the Basilica of Constantine, by P.M. Gauthier presents a reconstruction of the apsed central bay.

The drawings on this page depict the Napoleonic excavations of the Forum.

Overleaf: an 1815 print showing the most notable remains of ancient Rome.

106

AVANZI DEI PIU COSPICUI EDIFICJ ANTICHI DI ROMA E

Alla Nobile Donzella la Sig.ra Marchesa

DIACENZE COME SI OSSERVANO NELL'ANNO MDCCCXV

Giulia Zondadari già Chigi di Siena

reconstructions and the work of Theodor Mommsen (1817–1903). In 1845 this German scholar had determined the location of the *comitium,* the place where ancient Romans had held assemblies. After 1850 other excavations were begun: some were on the Palatine Hill, where the House of Livia, a part of the Temple of Apollo (thought at the time to be the Temple of the Victorious Jupiter), and remains of the imperial palaces were uncovered. On the Appian Way fresh excavations were entrusted to Luigi Canina.

The Tomb of Caecilia Metella on the Appian Way was built in the late 1st century BC. Its drum shape, like that of the Tomb of Augustus, attests to the influence of the Orient and Greece on Roman funerary architecture.

The queen of roads

Begun in the 4th century by Appius Claudius, who gave it his name, the Appian Way eventually crossed the Roman peninsula from Rome to Brindisi, a distance of 589 km. Lined with cypresses, pines and olive trees, it was flanked by temples, villas and funerary structures. (According to an old tradition, the ancients buried their dead outside the city, in places through which people travelled; the Romans, it was said, wished to show those

The tomb was popular with artists. For a long time it was called Capo di Bove, 'the Bull's Head', because of the bull's heads that adorn its frieze, a traditional decoration on funerary monuments.

who passed by that they, too, were mortal.) At the fifth milestone outside Rome the road divided at the place where the legendary Horatii were said to have fought the Curiatii. Their tombs, in the form of mounds, lay a little beyond, on the right side of the road.

In the Middle Ages nobles occupied and fortified some of the structures along the Appian Way, including the Tomb of Caecilia Metella, a mausoleum shaped like a tower that served as a keep for a massive fortified castle. Other remains were used as sources of building materials. Still others were simply abandoned, becoming hideouts for bandits. Renaissance artists – including Raphael and Michelangelo – appealed in vain for the Appian Way to be saved. By the 19th century, its outline was disappearing amid the ruined tombs.

Paved with slabs of basalt and bordered by footways of beaten earth, the Appian Way, stretching from Rome to the opposite side of the peninsula, was wide enough (4.10 m) to allow vehicles to pass in both directions. Every 7 or 10 Roman miles, travellers found relay posts, for changing horses, and an inn.

Luigi Canina, restorer of the Appian Way

The 1850 plan had several aims: to sort out the whole area around the road, to reveal the line of the road, and to uncover what was left of it. Three years of intensive work were devoted to the road's first section. Canina wrote very detailed commentaries and recorded the state of the road and its restoration in large engraved plates. He imagined the long series of tombs that stood on the site, some of them monumental and decorated with stucco and frescoes, others simple altars. In this way he described thousands of tombs along the first 16 km of the road: pyramid-shaped ones, round drumlike ones, or formal ones resembling temples. Doubts have been cast on Canina's reconstructions as a result of excavations made in our own century, but his plates give us an excellent idea of what those great consular roads must once have looked like leaving the gates of the capital and crossing the empire. Their common symbolic starting point was marked by the golden column that Augustus had placed in the center of the Forum.

The revival of Christian archaeology

The Greek and Roman gods and heroes of the ancient republic were no longer the only idols of the 19th

RELIQVIE DEL GRANDE MONVMENTO DENOMINATO CASAL ROTONDO

ESPOSIZIONE DELL'INTERA ARCHITETTVRA DEL GRANDE MONVMENTO
DI MESSALA CORVINO VLTIMATO DA M.VALERIO MESSALINO COTTA

The Appian Way was in use for several centuries, and was flanked by tombs whose variety of periods and forms explains the attraction the queen of roads had for travellers: little structures in the shape of temples, simple altars, tombs with podiums, exedrae with or without columns, and drumlike forms such as the Casal Rotondo (opposite and left, illustrations from Canina's *La Via Appia*), a tomb 35 m in diameter.

century. The field of archaeological exploration was now extended to the whole of the Mediterranean and to the Middle East. Such figures as the German scholar Heinrich Schliemann, the discoverer of Troy, and the great French Egyptologist Jean-François Champollion came to the fore. The Etruscan and Mesopotamian civilizations were unearthed. In Rome the catacombs were rediscovered.

The Catacombs of St Sebastian were known about at the beginning of the 19th century; but since Bosio's time, most of these underground cemeteries had largely been abandoned or even forgotten. A scholar, Giuseppe Marchi, was the first to draw Pope Gregory XVI's attention to the need to safeguard this evidence of Christian history. In 1841 Marchi was entrusted with their supervision, and in 1854 he was put in charge of the founding of the Christian Museum of the Lateran.

The catacombs are underground cemeteries where sanctuaries were later built near the crypts of the martyrs. On these two pages are illustrations of the catacombs from De' Rossi's *Underground Christian Rome.*

Giovanni Battista de' Rossi, the undisputed prince of underground Rome

At the same time, Giovanni Battista de' Rossi, a disciple of Marchi's, decided to make a precise map of the catacombs. He consulted a wide variety of traditional literary and ecclesiastical sources and medieval documents: itineraries, catalogues of relics, and catalogues of cemeteries. By cross-checking these

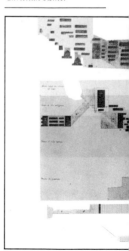

documents, De' Rossi believed he could determine the location of the crypt of St Sixtus, and, in that very location, he found the inscription ...NELIVS MARTYR. He knew from the texts that Pope Cornelius had been buried close to the grave of Sixtus (martyred in AD 258).

Prolonged excavation enabled him to find the crypt, as well as the whole of the Catacombs of St Callistus. De' Rossi then realized why the crypt had remained buried for so long: following many invasions, during which the tombs of the martyrs had been ransacked, in the 4th century Pope Damasus I and his successors had had wide staircases built in the underground galleries, wide enough for the pilgrims to descend directly to the sites they wanted to visit. Passages were cut into the sanctuaries to allow air and light to enter. With time, these structures collapsed, blocking the galleries and tunnels. Until De' Rossi's time, grave robbers and archaeologists had stopped at these heaps of earth, but he dug through them, passed on, and discovered the heart of the catacombs.

By following the same method, De' Rossi uncovered twenty-six catacombs, opening galleries that had lain buried for nearly ten centuries. In the underground

Cross sections of the catacombs (below).

basilicas ceremonies were again held, and pilgrims came. Pope Pius IX himself visited these famous places. Pictures spread throughout the world. Sacred art once again became a subject of study and admiration.

The religious fervour aroused by these discoveries, as well as the influence of the church, especially the Jesuits, might have become an obstacle to the scientific advance of Christian archaeology, but De' Rossi was able to convince scholars of his findings. He was invited to collaborate with Mommsen and J.H.W. Henzen on the publication of the great corpus of Latin inscriptions. For thirteen years, 1864–1877, he worked on his book, *Underground Christian Rome,* in which he examined the funerary practices of the first Christians and the very numerous graffiti found on the walls, and illustrated some of the most famous catacombs, including copies of their frescoes and inscriptions. Starting in 1863 De' Rossi edited the *Bulletin of Christian Archaeology.* By the end of his life he had published more than two hundred texts. After his death new discoveries continued to be made. There are now sixty-seven known catacombs in Rome.

The demanding and difficult work of the archaeologist: to excavate, interpret, classify, and inform

All the scholars of the period were busy classifying and defining their discipline, and those working on antiquity benefited from this great wave of rational thought. New methods of establishing correct editions of texts were devised; catalogues raisonnés of objects were published, as were the great collections of Greek and Latin

Pope Pius IX visits the 'Crypt of the Popes' with De' Rossi.

inscriptions, which were presented in topographical order. The museums also prepared thematic catalogues of their collections. The dissemination of information improved. Various publications presented accounts of recent discoveries and commented on them, while new associations financed further exploration.

Overleaf: tourists visit the catacombs: two different views, both of 1900.

The Roman Academy, founded in 1810, brought together archaeologists and amateurs, artists and clerics who aspired to be the heirs of Pomponius Laetus and the humanists. They organized lavish banquets and visited the ruins together.

The founding of the great archaeological institutes

The Institute of Archaeological Correspondence was created in 1829, at the initiative of archaeologists and artists, and with the support of kings Ludwig I of Bavaria and Frederick William III of Prussia. The institute published a bulletin and annals that describe discoveries made all over the world. For nearly forty years, the history of archaeology was linked to that institute; its international role dwindled only as a result of the Franco-Prussian War of 1870. From then on it was controlled solely by the Germans and became the German Archaeological Institute. Its activities extended to Athens, Cairo and Istanbul. In 1873 the French founded another institution, the French School of Rome.

By this time the progress made in archaeology could no longer be questioned. Even if the explorers were sometimes amateurs, and even though the antiquarian spirit persisted, there were now also genuine scholars at work on genuine excavation projects.

Archaeology, however, needed to develop new methods, in-depth excavations, and a historical approach. Shortly before his death, in his book *Rome in the Year 1838,* Nibby wrote: 'Nothing remains on the surface of the ground. But I, who was born amid these ruins and who have lived in them, I can testify that in all the cellars of all the houses of this region, and in many of the walls, there is evidence to prove that if one were to excavate the ground and demolish the houses, one would find exceptionally important information concerning the ancient topography of Rome and the history of the arts.'

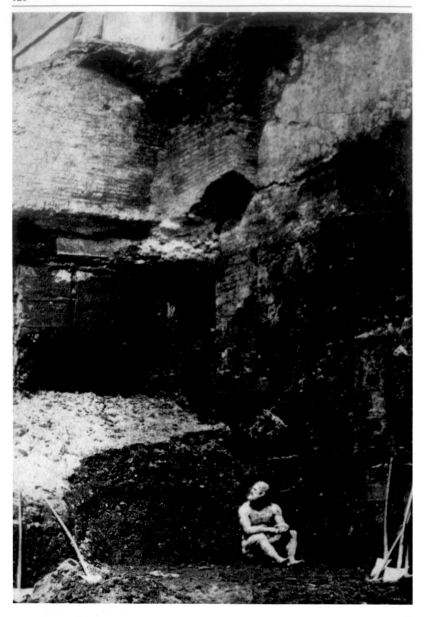

In the 20th century archaeology entered the modern era and found its methodology. After centuries of isolated excavations and discoveries limited to the republican and imperial periods, the earlier Rome – the Rome of the kings – arose from the depths of the earth, gradually revealing the mysterious origins of the city.

CHAPTER 6
FROM ONE MYTH TO ANOTHER

The discovery of the *Seated Gladiator* (opposite), 1885, and the statue today.

"I have never experienced an impression as extraordinary as when I saw that almost barbarian athlete who seemed to be awakening from a thousand-year-long sleep after long and terrible struggles."
Rodolfo Lanciani

In the wake of Italian unification, major work began on the Esquiline, one of Rome's seven hills, to create a new district; at this time many remains of the houses, villas and tombs were discovered. In this 1871 photograph, which shows a site being excavated near the so-called Temple of Minerva Medica, the workers have revealed part of an ancient brick wall.

In 1861 Italy began the process of national unification, and in 1870 Rome was declared the capital of the new country. The new monarchy wanted a capital city that was worthy of the ancient city and the city of the popes. In this 'third Rome', everything still had to be built: neither the populace nor the new administration could move into the palaces or the hovels. An unimagined Rome appeared beneath the spade and the pickaxe, but many remains disappeared beneath modern buildings. Some old districts – a large part of the medieval city, including several monasteries and many palaces and famous villas – were wiped from the map.

Below: objects found during the construction of the new city, photographed in 1874.

'They are building furiously,' wrote the indignant German historian Ferdinand Gregorovius, 'neighbourhoods and hills are being turned upside down.... Every hour, I see a piece of ancient Rome falling.... The old city is disappearing....' All that the archaeologist Rodolfo

Lanciani produced in reply, in defence of the
construction projects, was a list of the discoveries made
between 1870 and 1885: '705 amphorae, 2360 lamps,
1824 inscriptions, 77 columns of pink marble, 313
pieces of columns, 157 capitals, 18 sarcophagi, 36,679
gold, silver, and bronze coins.'

In fact, never had so much been destroyed or
discovered since the late 16th century under Sixtus V's
rule – and now without the slightest thought being given
to urban design. On the Esquiline, Quirinal, and
Viminal hills, Roman houses containing frescoes,
mosaics, and sculptures – even a whole necropolis –
came to light. Bas-reliefs, terra-cottas, domestic objects
and statues, including a bronze Bacchus with long hair,
an armless Apollo, and a life-size head of Aphrodite, were
recovered from the Tiber. When the river embankments
were built, the gardens of the Villa Farnesina were
excavated, revealing a villa containing one of the finest
series of frescoes and stuccos found up to that time.
What emotion there must have been in seeing the myth
of Phaëthon, the legend of Dionysus, and genre paintings
glorifying love all emerging from the depths of the earth.

A fresco (above) and a
stucco relief (below)
found near the Farnesina.

Everything about these remains was extremely fine, especially the stuccos, where every gesture, every piece of clothing, looked like a miraculous fossil.

Italian archaeology reaches maturity

These discoveries, the history of which is very similar to those of previous centuries, enriched the 'Museo delle Terme', which was installed in 1889 in the Baths of Diocletian. Italy's King Victor Emmanuel II was genuinely concerned with protecting the artistic heritage of his country. In 1870 he founded an official body charged with administering the excavations and conserving the monuments of the province of Rome. In 1875 he created the Italian School of Archaeology. It was modelled on the French and German institutes and encouraged the resumption of the excavations in the

'monumental centre' of Rome. On the Palatine, what was known as the Stadium of Domitian was uncovered; in the Colosseum, the whole of the underground passages and chambers was revealed. In the Forum, first the central area was cleared, and then the ground of the entire site was levelled. 'From February to April 1882,' wrote Lanciani, 'more than 10,200 cubic meters of earth were removed and cleared, and 2800 square meters of ancient ground were uncovered.'

Twenty-six inscriptions and a large number of remains of monuments were found.... For the first time since the fall of the Roman Empire, one could walk along the entire length of the Via Sacra from where it started to the Capitoline.'

Had the ancients told the truth?

In June 1899, in the northwestern part of the Forum, Giacomo Boni uncovered a black marble slab that was almost square (3 by 4 m), surrounded by a white line.

Though trained as an architect, Giacomo Boni (1859–1925, left) was especially interested in geology and construction techniques. Before him, archaeologists were topographers and scholars whose excavations were guided by texts and who delegated fieldwork. Boni took up the spade and pickaxe himself and thus became a pioneer of active archaeology. In contrast to his peers, he believed archaeology served to reconstruct the history of a site from its origins, a goal that could be attained only by stratigraphy – uncovering the different layers systematically. Boni's contemporaries retained almost nothing of his lessons. The stratigraphic method was not applied systematically to Classical sites until the 1960s.

In 1875 excavations made around the Colosseum revealed underground service passages that were used during the games. In ancient times they were covered by an enormous wooden platform. Here, the inside of the Colosseum before and after the excavations.

The ancient authors spoke of the existence of a black stone in the Forum, the *lapis niger*. According to some, it marked the location of Romulus' tomb; others said that it was the tomb of Faustulus, Romulus' foster father, and still others the tomb of Hostilian, the third king of Rome.

Hoping to reach this mysterious tomb, Boni dug deeper: under the marble appeared an archaic group made up of what seemed to be a kind of tomb (it was, in fact, an altar) and a stela that was covered with inscriptions. The text, which is written partly in boustrophedon (a system of writing from left to right and then right to left, and so on), is still difficult to comprehend: the letters are too close to each other, and it is barely possible to make out a few words. Only the first sentence has been completely deciphered: 'Whoever violates this sacred place shall be destined for the infernal gods.' The appearance of this prohibition, presumably a sacred archaic law from the 6th century BC,

In August 1899 it was decided to clear the whole of the space that stretched from the Temple of Antoninus and Faustina (above centre in the photograph) to the Curia. An enormous amount of earth was removed, and a large number of houses were demolished. The Basilica Aemilia, a building dating from the republican period, was revealed. Here Guido Baccelli, a government minister, visits the excavations.

associated with sanctuaries dedicated to
Vulcan, the Roman god of fire, unleashed a
historical debate.

Germans against Italians: patriotic archaeology

For several years, German historians had
questioned the value of the ancient texts,
especially those of Livy, concerning the
origins of the city. Opposing this so-called
hypercritical school were most of the Italians,
who were 'traditionalists'. They believed in
the texts.

The black stone appeared to prove the
Italians right: did it not
confirm the traditional story
of the founding of Rome?
Debate was acrimonious
and had an effect on public
opinion, further dividing
the Italians from the
Germans.

The controversy was
revived in 1902 and again in 1907, with
the successive discoveries of two
necropoli from the 9th and 8th
centuries BC near the Temple of
Antoninus and Faustina and on the
Quirinal. At the same time,
Boni was uncovering the bases of huts
dating from the same period on the
Palatine. The debate did not last long,
however, even though the new
revelations corroborated the statements
of the ancients on the settlement of the hills in very early
times. Because their training was inadequate and their
methods insufficient, the archaeologists were not ready to
undertake difficult excavations. Boni himself preferred
not to take his investigations any further, even though he
was the only archaeologist who would have been able to
do so, since he was the first one to apply the stratigraphic
method to historical excavation.

The discovery of the
lapis niger near the
Arch of Septimius
Severus attracted crowds.
Here Baccelli is depicted
inspecting the dig.

A 20th-century antiquarian: Rodolfo Lanciani

At this time, archaeologists still largely devoted their
time to topography. Lanciani studied the Forma Urbis,
the marble map from the 3rd century. He drew up a new
archaeological map of the city using a scale of 1:1000
and produced extremely erudite plates that detailed the
chronology of the discoveries made since the 15th
century. Lanciani belonged to the old antiquarian school,
which was less concerned with analysis than with
description and assembly; but for this map he also used
his own remarkable knowledge of the city. Lanciani liked
to explore the least-known parts of the Roman
Campagna, as people had in the 16th century. One can
tell that he really saw Rome stone by stone. Indeed, he
inspected all the excavation sites at a time when on all
sides the city was being gutted and turned upside-down,
once again giving up its soul.

By this point it was photographs rather than drawings
that archaeologists were bringing back with them
from their lengthy investigations. At the time they
barely understood the importance of photography,
which Boni had used in the Forum, shooting from an
aerostatic balloon. The English archaeologist John
Henry Parker had been the first to employ this new
method for scholarly purposes in the 1870s.

The cult of *Romanità*

In 1911 Lanciani organized a great exhibition to
celebrate the fiftieth anniversary of Italian unity. Here
the most important archaeological discoveries were put
on show – with pride of place going to the Augustus
statue from the Prima Porta. On the eve of the Libyan
expedition in the Turkish-Italian War, the monarchy
considered it important to demonstrate that Roman
civilization was still thriving, as shown by the roads,
bridges, and monuments that were still visible in the
landscape of the former Roman provinces. The myth of
Rome, which had served political ambitions since the
Middle Ages, thus survived in modern Italy. Italian unity
and Roman identity were celebrated together. Fascism
gave this idea its most extreme expression.

Born in London in
1806, John Henry
Parker (below) was a
scholar fascinated by the
history of architecture. In
1866 he decided to
photograph all the major
ancient monuments
systematically.

The major work of Rodolfo Lanciani (1845–1929), *The Forma Urbis,* shows Rome as it appeared in three eras: antiquity, the Middle Ages, and the late 19th century. His plan of the Forum is still quite accurate, apart from a few details, in spite of recent discoveries that have revealed a number of early remains between the Atrium Vestae and the Arch of Titus.

Left: Parker's photograph looking through the Arch of Titus towards the Colosseum and the Arch of Constantine.

'Five years from now', Mussolini declared on 31 December 1925, 'Rome must appear in all its splendour: immense, ordered, and as powerful as it was at the time of the first empire, that of Augustus.' The impetus given to Classical studies and to Roman history, the eagle that symbolized the regime, and the insistence on reviving Latin as a 'speakable language' were all aspects of the exaltation of *Romanità* – Romanness. It was hardly surprising that the Fascists wanted archaeology to play an essential role in their propaganda. Giglioli, the chief archaeologist of Mussolini's regime, evoked 'the development of archaeological research in relation to the historical and national aims of Fascism'. He gave historians the task of demonstrating the continuity of the history of Rome, the permanence of the Roman

"One order from Benito Mussolini, and everything that is considered unworthy disappears from the map," commented a journal of the period.

nation, and the grandeur it had enjoyed since its origin.

With a large team of archaeologists, Mussolini planned a vast programme of excavations. In the mass of projects, two groups illustrate in the clearest possible way the political use of history, a concept he was fond of. On the one hand, there was the restoration of the Augustan city, and on the other, the excavation of the Imperial Forums and of Ostia, associated with the construction of the Via del Mare, the road to the sea. This road was the symbol and axis of the extension of Rome towards the Mediterranean. As in previous centuries, the archaeological programmes were linked with the rebuilding of the city. Mussolini ordered both destruction and construction. Once again, the small squares and narrow streets of Rome were destroyed to bring to the surface 'that civilization that is buried but not dead.'

A bove left: the Roman eagle (here on a cameo of 27 AD) was taken up as a symbol by Mussolini. Above: a copy of the Prima Porta *Augustus* used as a Fascist memorial.

T he pickaxe in this photograph (left) symbolizes perfectly the way the Fascists massacred the city. Here, Mussolini himself wields the axe to open the excavation of the Via dell'Impero.

The Ara Pacis (opposite and below) consisted of an enclosed podium reached via a staircase. The altar is inside the enclosure. Important members of the imperial family are depicted on the southern frieze, details of which are shown at left. Agrippa, Augustus' son-in-law, is the figure to the right.

The 2000th anniversary of Augustus: Fascist Rome celebrates Imperial Rome

After the excavation of the Forum of Augustus, which was done casually, without any measurements or records, the celebration of Augustus culminated in 1937–8, on the 2000th anniversary of his birth. His mausoleum was restored and isolated by the creation of the Piazza Augusto Imperatore; the Altar of Peace, the Ara Pacis, was reconstructed and set up nearby, close to the river. Last and most important of all, in 1937 there was an extremely spectacular exhibition, the 'Mostra Augustea della Romanità'.

The organizers of 1937 were much more ambitious than Rodolfo Lanciani had been in 1911: they wanted this to be the greatest exhibition of the century. They commissioned maps, drawings, photographs, plaster casts, and, most important, more than three hundred models of famous monuments from all over the empire. A great model or relief map of Rome celebrated the magnificence of the imperial city at the beginning of the 4th century.

Erected in 9 BC, the Ara Pacis was one of the most important symbols of Augustan imperial propaganda, exalting Rome's universal dominion, its divine origin, and the peace it imposed – the *pax romana*. Various fragments of the structure had been found in the 16th and 19th centuries but it was not until 1937–8 that it was fully excavated. On the occasion of Augustus' 2000th anniversary, the altar was re-erected near Augustus' mausoleum beside the Tiber and protected by a structure of glass and concrete. The terms of the emperor's will were inscribed on the walls of the monument. It was dedicated on 23 September 1938.

Greatness rediscovered

On 23 September 1937 the 'Mostra Augustea della Romanità' opened in the Palace of Expositions on the Via Nazionale, featuring a display of photographs, drawings and models. The materials from the exposition were to have been reused for the Universal Exposition in Rome in 1942, which was supposed to celebrate the conquest of Ethiopia and the twentieth anniversary of the regime. A whole district in southern Rome was set aside for the exposition, but work was interrupted by World War II and the defeat of Fascism and was not completed until the 1950s. The Museum of Roman Civilization was opened in 1955; today it houses the materials from the 1911 and 1937 expositions.

Left: a reconstruction of the Colosseum.

Pages 136–7: part of the great model of ancient Rome showing the Circus Maximus, the Palatine and the Forum area.

Pages 138–9: a watercolour reconstruction of the Roman Forum.

Many other countries contributed to this exhibition as well, creating a sense of solidarity with Mussolini.

In addition, the exhibition was a scholarly success. It was the first-ever assemblage of material that had been scattered all over the world. However, in his opening speech Giglioli did not hide the political role of the enterprise: *Romanità* was proclaimed the mother of all peoples, and Mussolini was acclaimed as its defender, the guarantor of glories to come.

Mussolini, of course, was not satisfied with such gestures. He demanded a grander stroke: he wanted to give Rome its opening to the sea at Ostia. To link the city with the coast he needed a glorious road. It ran past the restored Imperial Forums and was punctuated by five maps showing the Roman conquests from the beginning up to the Fascist empire.

The Theatre of Ostia (with a capacity of three thousand) was restored in the 1930s. At the back of the orchestra and the semicircular stage, on the site of the arcaded portico, marble fragments found on the site have been installed.

An assessment of Fascist archaeology

Mussolini also had the site of Ostia excavated. The ancient port of Rome had already been explored in the 18th century. Carlo Fea had sent fifty prisoners there to carry out basic excavation, but he soon had to give that up, as the region was too marshy. Work had begun again later, for a longer period of time, under Pius IX, revealing statues and considerable remains of paintings. In 1910 the archaeologist Vaglicri discovered a winged statue of Minerva Victrix there; the fact that she was 'victorious' was, at the time, thought to be a good omen for the new state. But Ostia was not truly revealed until 1938–42.

It must be said, however, that the archaeologist in charge, Guido Galza, made serious mistakes on the project. Rushing to meet the deadline of the 1942 Universal Exposition, he exposed only the level dating

The Via Severiana (above) crosses the necropolis of the Isola Sacra, near Ostia. It was 10.5 m wide, and divided into one section for vehicles and another for pedestrians, riders, and funeral processions.

This mosaic (left) was discovered in the Baths of Neptune at Ostia.

from the 2nd century AD. The more recent layers disappeared without being recorded, and the oldest layers remained buried.

Yet the exploration of Ostia was an important landmark in the history of Roman architecture, revealing for the first time the famous granaries, called *horrea,* and the *insulae,* the ancestors of modern apartment buildings. In addition, the excavation of a necropolis and the *mithrea,* small chapels where the god Mithras was worshipped, shed new light on the religious life of the 2nd and 3rd centuries AD and on the popularity of the Oriental cults that were the rivals of Christianity.

Traces of Romulus?

Like previous periods, the 20th century has yielded and continues to yield a number of masterpieces. Might Roman soil be inexhaustible? So much still remains to be excavated that it is truly impossible to estimate its riches. We still know very little, for example, about the Campus Martius. Archaeologists have to be satisfied with hypotheses formed on the basis of texts and the Forma Urbis of the 3rd century. The Circus of Flaminius, the three temples of Jupiter, Juno and Hercules, and the Theatre of Bacchus are all still hidden. We know quite precisely that, for example, we would find the ruins of the Temple of Jupiter beneath the church of Santa Maria in Campitelli. But the piling up of material over the centuries has been continuous in that district of the city, and only the Portico of Octavia reflects some of its former splendour. One would have to dig very deeply indeed.

On other sites, very early material is being unearthed. Signs of life from as early as the 8th century BC, discovered by Boni on the hills, and the archaic temple discovered under Sant'Omobono around 1930 attesting to the presence of the Etruscan kings in the 6th century BC, seem to confirm the accounts of the ancient historians. The Palatine Hill may well have yielded up one of its last secrets when, in October 1988, an

The emblem of Rome is the sacred animal of the god Mars, the she-wolf. According to legend, the wolf saved the founders of the city Romulus and Remus, sons of Mars and the Vestal Virgin Rhea Silvia.

archaeologist found the traces of an archaic wall on the edge of the Forum. It may be the one thought to have been built in the 8th century BC to define the sacred space of the city.

Until the 20th century the discoveries were related to the imperial period or to the end of the republic. Now it is archaic Rome, the Rome of the kings, that is being revealed little by little, as though archaeology were getting closer to the beginning of things as we get further from them in time. The Eternal City continues to reveal its secrets.

This archaic bronze statue of the *She-Wolf*, dating from the 5th century BC, did not originally include the twins; they were added by a sculptor in the 15th century. Its first location is unknown, but Dante saw it at the Lateran Palace. It was moved from there to the Capitol in 1471.

Overleaf: discovery of a statue in the 1950s (left) and excavations near the Meta Sudans in 1813 (right).

DOCUMENTS

The city under threat

Throughout Roman history the theme of Rome's destruction has been at the heart of people's preoccupation with the city. The need for protective measures has always been urgent.

Foreign invaders were not the only destroyers of the city. The indifference and carelessness of Romans themselves — centuries of pillage by emperors and aristocrats and ordinary citizens — played just as major a role in its devastation. Repeated appeals were addressed by the emperors to the magistrates of Rome, urging them to protect public buildings, but the sheer number of edicts proves that they were generally not effective.

EMPERORS LEO AND MAJORIAN, THE AUGUST, TO EMILIAN, PREFECT OF THE CITY OF ROME

In our governance of the state, we wish to correct the fact, which we have long condemned, that people are able to change the appearance of a venerable city. For it is clearly evident that the public buildings which form the entire adornment of the city of Rome are being gradually destroyed in response to the punishable suggestion of the

R uins on the Palatine, one of the seven hills of Rome and the centre of political and social life during the empire.

Detail of a plan of ancient Rome.

Offices of the City. Citing the fallacious pretext of an urgent need for freestone for the construction of a public building, the admirable structures of ancient buildings are dismantled. For the restoration of some small building, large ones are being destroyed. This provides opportunities for anyone putting up a private building, by the grace of the appointed magistrates of the city, to take the necessary materials from public sites and to transport them to some other place, when in fact they form part of the city's splendour and one should therefore preserve them out of civic conscience, even where the buildings are in need of repair.

That is why we decree by this general law that nobody shall destroy or damage the whole set of buildings, that is to say, the temples and monuments founded by our forefathers, which were built for the public's use or enjoyment; this is to be enforced so that a magistrate who decides to make such an act shall have to pay a fine of fifty pounds of gold. As for employees and bookkeepers obeying his orders and not daring to resist him on their own initiative, they expose themselves to punishment by beating, and they shall also have their hands amputated – those hands with which they profane the monuments of the ancestors, when they should be preserved.

As for the places that until now individuals have claimed for themselves – a piece of mischief that must be abolished – we forbid that anything be removed from them, since, in fact, they continue to form part of the public property, and we desire that they be repaired and have restored to them those parts that have been removed, the authorization to make a claim to them having henceforth been suspended.

If urgent and overwhelming reasons make it necessary to dismantle any section, either because of the building of another public work or in order that vital repair work be undertaken, we prescribe that the issue be submitted, with all applicable information, to the venerable Senate. If after due deliberation it should consider that such action needs to be taken, the case is to be referred to our own benevolence in order that whatever we find to be beyond repair, we may order that it, at least, be transferred and made to adorn another public building, O Emilian, very dear and very affectionate father.

For these reasons, Your Illustrious Highness, please be so kind as to publish, by displaying edicts, this very salutary constitution, in order that decisions that we have taken with forethought in the interest of the

Eternal City be observed with the appropriate submission and devotion.

Signed at Ravenna,
11 July AD 458

The disappearance of a cultural heritage

In the course of the Middle Ages, a very large quantity of marble was burned in special limekilns and then reused as building material. Archaeologists such as Rodolfo Lanciani discovered a number of these limekilns in the 19th century.

A limekiln was found in the Palace of Tiberius on the Palatine Hill…in 1869. It was filled to the brim with fine works of art, some calcined, some intact. Among the latter were the veiled bust of Claudius now in the Museo delle Terme; a head of Nero; three caryatids in nero antico [an ornamental black marble]; the exquisite little statuette of an ephebus in black basalt…; a head of Harpocrates, and other minor fragments.

In February 1883, in the excavations on the south side of the Atrium of Vesta, a pile of marble was found about fourteen feet long, nine feet wide, and seven feet high [4.30 / 2.75 / 2.10 m]. It was wholly made up of statues of the *Vestales maximae,* some unbroken, others in fragments. The statues and fragments had been carefully packed together, leaving as few interstices as possible between them, and the spaces formed by the curves of the bodies were filled in with chips. There were eight nearly perfect statues, and we were agreeably surprised to find among the broken ones the lower part of the lovely seated Vesta with the footstool, which, alas, is now hardly recognizable, owing to the number of years it has been left

View of an 18th-century workshop for restoring antique statues.

exposed in the dampest corner of the atrium. There were present at this remarkable discovery, which took place at 6:30 AM on 9 February, only four people besides the workmen – the Crown Prince of Prussia, afterward the Emperor Frederick III, Dr Henzen, one of my colleagues, and myself. I distinctly remember how the prince, then in the full vigour of health and strength, helped the workmen to raise the masses of marble and to set the statues up against the wall of the atrium. That was the golden age of Roman excavation, and we recall it as if it were a dream! These beautiful statues had been piled into a regular oblong, like a cord of wood, by some diggers of marbles, who had carefully filled the spaces between the statues as they lay side by side, in order that no empty spaces might be left. By what fortunate accident these sculptures were preserved it is difficult to guess; but one thing at least is certain – a great quantity of other marbles belonging to the House of the Vestals must have perished by fire. Two kilns and two deposits of lime and of charcoal were found in the course of the same excavations.

Rodolfo Lanciani
The Destruction of Ancient Rome
1901

Poggio Bracciolini's contemplation of Rome

The contemplation of ruins inspired more than one vocation. Surveying the misfortunes of the city in 1430, Poggio Bracciolini (1380–1459) came to understand his passionate interest in Graeco-Roman antiquity. Edward Gibbon (1737–94) included a description of this moment in his masterwork on the fall of the Roman Empire.

In the last days of Pope Eugenius the Fourth, two of his servants, the learned Poggius and a friend, ascended the Capitoline hill, reposed themselves among the ruins of columns and temples, and viewed from that commanding spot the wide and various prospect of desolation. The place and the object gave ample scope for moralising on the vicissitudes of fortune, which spares neither man nor the proudest of his works, which buries empires and cities in a common grave; and it was agreed that, in proportion to her former greatness, the fall of Rome was the more awful and deplorable. 'Her primeval state, such as she might appear in a remote age when Evander entertained the stranger of Troy, has

been delineated by the fancy of Virgil. This Tarpeian rock was then a savage and solitary thicket: in the time of the poet it was crowned with the golden roofs of a temple; the temple is overthrown, the gold has been pillaged, the wheel of fortune has accomplished her revolution, and the sacred ground is again disfigured with thorns and brambles. The hill of the Capitol, on which we sit, was formerly the head of the Roman Empire, the citadel of the earth, the terror of kings; illustrated by the footsteps of so many triumphs, enriched with the spoils and tributes of so many nations. This spectacle of the world, how it is fallen! how changed! how defaced! The path of victory is obliterated by vines, and the benches of the senators are concealed by a dunghill. Cast your eyes on the Palatine hill, and seek among the shapeless and enormous fragments the marble

H istorian Gian Francesco Poggio Bracciolini, sometimes known as Poggius.

theatre, the obelisks, the colossal statues, the porticoes of Nero's palace: Survey the other hills of the city, the vacant space is interrupted only by ruins and gardens. The forum of the Roman people, where they assembled to enact their laws and elect their magistrates, is now enclosed for the cultivation of pot-herbs, or thrown open for the reception of swine and buffaloes. The public and private edifices, that were founded for eternity, lie prostrate, naked, and broken, like the limbs of a mighty giant; and the ruin is the more visible, from the stupendous relics that have survived the injuries of time and fortune.'

These relics are minutely described by Poggius, one of the first who raised his eyes from the monuments of legendary to those of classic superstition. 1. Besides a bridge, an arch, a sepulchre, and the pyramid of Cestius, he could discern, of the age of the republic, a double row of vaults in the salt-office of the Capitol, which were inscribed with the name and munificence of Catulus. 2. Eleven temples were visible in some degree, from the perfect form of the Pantheon to the three arches and a marble column of the temple of Peace, which Vespasian erected after the civil wars and the Jewish triumph. 3. Of the number, which he rashly defines, of seven *thermae*, or public baths, none were sufficiently entire to represent the use and distribution of the several paths; but those of Diocletian and Antoninus Caracalla still retained the

The ruined side of the Colosseum.

The Septizonium was built at the beginning of the 3rd century AD by Septimius Severus. Large parts of the building survived, but in the 16th century Sixtus V had its remains demolished.

titles of the founders, and astonished the curious spectator, who, in observing their solidity and extent, the variety of marbles, the size and multitude of the columns, compared the labour and expense with the use and importance. Of the baths of Constantine, of Alexander, of Domitian, or rather of Titus, some vestige might yet be found.

4. The triumphal arches of Titus, Severus, and Constantine, were entire, both the structure and the inscriptions: A falling fragment was honoured with the name of Trajan; and two arches, then extant, in the Flaminian way, have been ascribed to the base memory of Faustina and Gallienus. 5. After the wonder of the [Colosseum], Poggius might have overlooked a small amphitheatre of brick, most probably for the use of the praetorian camp: The theatres of Marcellus and Pompey were occupied in a great measure by public and private buildings; and in the Circus, Agonalis and Maximus, little more than the situation and the form could be investigated. 6. The columns of Trajan and Antonine were still erect, but the Egyptian obelisks were broken or buried. A people of gods and heroes, the workmanship of art, was reduced to one equestrian figure of gilt brass and to five marble statues, of which the most conspicuous were the two horses of Phidias and Praxiteles. 7. The two mausoleums or sepulchres of Augustus and Hadrian could not totally be lost; but the former was only visible as a mound of earth, and the latter, the castle of St. Angelo, had acquired the name and appearance of a modern fortress. With the addition of some separate and nameless columns, such were the remains of the ancient city; for the marks of a more recent structure might be detected in the walls, which formed a circumference of ten miles, including three hundred and seventy-five turrets, and opened into the country by thirteen gates.

Edward Gibbon,
*The Decline and Fall
of the Roman Empire*, 1776–88

The defence of the Appian Way

Ranuccio Bianchi Bandinelli (1900–75) always defended the integrity of Rome's artistic heritage. This great archaeologist, a specialist in Etruscan art, art history, and theory, who was the director general of antiquities and fine arts in Rome from 1945 to 1947, spearheaded a movement that arose at the end of World War II calling for the protection of the ruins. He proposed, for example, that great archaeological parks be created along the Appian Way.

There are few places, not only in Italy, but in the whole world, that had as much evocative and suggestive power as the Appian Way in Rome, outside the Gate of St Sebastian. In its monuments, we read some remarkable pages of ancient history, from the end of the Roman Republic to the end of the empire, to the beginnings of Christianity and to the legends that go with it (the catacombs and the 'Quo Vadis' chapel are on this road). The view we have of the walls and of the Gate of St. Sebastian is still the same as that which, for two thousand years, those born in the Mezzogiorno had of the city of Rome, the centre of the Western world. After that time all of this would be destroyed and submerged beneath a flood of houses, disappearing quite simply because of a frenzy of speculation.

There are laws that protect the artistic and historic heritage, as well as the landscape. But laws are inert and impotent if there is a lack of real will to ensure that they are respected. In this case, as in a hundred others, the fault cannot be attributed to bureaucratic inertia: It lies much higher up, at the level of the government officials and, at a much higher level, in the ruling class.

It is surely symptomatic that when the alarm was sounded concerning the destruction of the Appian Way, not a single organ of the mighty middle-class press chose to champion the cause. In a hundred similar cases nobody chose to react. The whole of our incomparable artistic and cultural heritage is threatened with destruction: In the villas of the Veneto, rooms covered with Tiepolo's frescoes are being turned into stables; the Italian cities that are celebrated throughout the world as masterpieces of beauty and as the witnesses of first-rate popular culture are rapidly being transformed into something hybrid, vulgar, noisy, and colonial, like some cities in the interior of South America. (Already tourists flocking to visit the monuments are obliged to flee as soon as they can these cities that do so little to welcome them.) The ruins and remains of our old Etruscan cities, which, in terms of scholarship, are irreplaceable, are disappearing beneath the wheels of the tractors of the Ente Maremma, sacrificed to a demagogic and purely fraudulent agrarian 'reform.'

One could fill an entire volume with the evidence of the attacks that are successfully being mounted against the Italian artistic heritage. It would be pointless to counterbalance it with another volume of 'rescue projects' carried out by the department of the arts and by other institutes whose mission it is to safeguard the cultural heritage: We know perfectly well that these organizations are doing what they can, sometimes in quite heroic working conditions. Every

The paving of the Appian Way.

superintendent could tell numerous stories about the pressure exerted on him by the authorities, especially by the church, to allow the laws safeguarding the cultural heritage to be overlooked and about the way in which his attempts at resistance meet with less and less support from the central authorities.

The fact is that the safeguarding of the artistic and historical heritage is one of those banners that the middle classes held high when they were rising but which they have now allowed to fall. It is one of those banners that the vanguard of the working class, the rising ruling class, now has to pick up and hold up high. It alone can fight effectively today, including for that banner; and it will certainly find at its side many of the best representatives of the middle class, who are suffering because of what is happening but do not have the courage or the strength to fight it.

The laws and the institutes created in the past have become obsolete in the face of the attacks of the most rapacious speculators who are mounting the assault, encouraged and supported by those occupying the highest positions. The only law they know is that of lucre, of money; clerical demagogy and hypocrisy play their part. What else can one expect from the ruling class, which does not want to lead any more but merely to fill its own pockets?

A director general of the fine arts, who insisted that the distribution of a few administrators who are the directors of the departments for the protection of our cultural heritage be economically rationalized, tried to demonstrate that a few years later there would hardly be anyone left in Italy to whom one could entrust the country's artistic heritage. The best people, he said, were abandoning a difficult career, crammed with responsibilities, badly paid, and deprived of the moral support of the ruling classes.

A minister of national education in one of the De Gasperi governments replied cynically that no minister would ever take the problem seriously since there were so few of them that 'they do not represent an electoral force'! Clearly, for this minister, the artistic heritage could quietly be reduced to ruins. Even on this occasion, the man appeared as a typical representative of the leading groups of his party by virtue of his lack of culture and his lack of any living link with Italian reality, a link that makes us really love our country.

However, I would not wish to mislead my readers into believing that I am being motivated here by some fetishistic cult of what is old, antique, and covered in dust. That is not the case at all; the demands of contemporary life and, above all, the need the popular Italian masses have to see their living conditions improve, make necessary, especially in the larger cities, transformations that have to be accommodated; yet it is not really those transformations that are changing the face of the Appian Way, for if the inhabitants of the shacks are certainly being evicted, they will obviously not go and live in the private villas that are being built along it. Cities have to change in appearance since they are living organisms; wanting to stop this transformation would be like wanting to stop the growth of a human being and to prevent him from changing from the beautiful child that he was into a plain old man, something we can all experience. What counts is the fostering of a consciousness of the need to build new things while intelligently respecting the old; for every old house that one destroys is an open door on history that is closed forever. Before deciding to close it, one must reflect. What counts is removing the criterion of speculation, which is the only one respected today and which has already destroyed some of the cities in our country that are most famous for their beauty.

The beauty of Italian cities is not the result of a charming piece of luck but almost always of a precise will, of directives followed by generations of city governments, the direct expression of the people. Perhaps the most typical example of this will and continuity can be found in the documents of the medieval city of Siena, in which one finds, from the mid-13th to the mid-14th centuries, a whole series of statutes and decrees setting out the building standards for the improvement of the city and giving details of facilities offered to those who contribute to such improvements; the city of Siena is today one of the most precious urban monuments of the past, an object of admiration and study for the whole world. In Verona, in the statutes of 1276, it says that no authority or office may start building without the consent of the people's council and the agreement of the 'Offices of Ornamentation.' The Italian people are still aware of this cultural heritage, but this awareness has to be defined, made widely known, and supported if it is to become active.

The problem is not an easy one; indeed, it is often extremely difficult. That is why we must examine it very carefully. During the Fascist period, the frenzy of real-estate speculation was disguised beneath a quite inconsistent rhetoric, which led to the disruption of the urban fabric of Rome and of other cities in the name of the 'renewal of imperial goals' and to the demolition of old parts of the city because of a hatred of the 'picturesque, which we do not like', or in homage to what remained of Marinetti's Futurism – one of the rare cultural experiences that was also extremely provincial, of the then leader of the country. There were occasions when the organizations safeguarding the cultural heritage were desperately trying to save a historic building and were attempting to gain some time, and the building was demolished during the night by armed gangs led by some potbellied Fascist official who was full of juvenile daring. Then, as today, the typical response of the Fascist mentality to these difficult questions is a confrontation of power. But today, there isn't even any appeal to rhetoric; today, the agents of real-estate speculation, who invest money at a profit of at least twenty-five percent, are very clever in finding the most bizarre devices in order to evade financial and technical controls. Certain of their impunity and of the complicity of those in power, who help them to evade the obligations set down by the laws regulating urban development and the limits that may be imposed by the laws protecting the artistic heritage and the landscape, they launch an open attack. One of the great scars inflicted upon the Appian Way was the building of the Pia Casa Santa Rosa, for which it was permitted that all the rules be broken 'out of deference for the charitable institution.' It was probably out of deference for that distinguished character that the mayor of Rome was authorized to build a house on a plot of land that the regulatory plan had destined to become a public garden.

No will, other than that of the most advanced and responsible sector of the people, can end this destruction and stop these people from doing what they are so eager to do.

Ranuccio Bianchi Bandinelli,
Rome: The Centre of Power, 1970

Remains of tombs along the Appian Way.

Piranesi, the archaeologist

The appearance of Roman Antiquities *by Giovanni Battista Piranesi in 1756 made this poetically-minded printmaker a pioneer of Roman archaeology. His vision of antiquity impressed the whole of Europe in his lifetime and is still a potent force today. The exceptional success of this work is explained by Piranesi's profound knowledge of engineering and architecture, combined with an outstandingly powerful imagination.*

Piranesi's etching of the mausoleum of Caecilia Metella.

"While stands the Coliseum, Rome shall stand;./ When falls the Coliseum, Rome shall fall, / And when

"...Rome falls – the world." Lord Byron, 1818

T his frontispiece to the second volume of Piranesi's *Roman Antiquities* reflects his enormous interest i nerary architecture, especially in the tombs of the Appian Way, imaginatively reconstructed here.

The journey to Rome

Rome has always fascinated foreigners. For centuries pilgrims, humanists, artists and statesmen have rushed to its gates, eager to admire its legendary wonders. Whether they were delighted or disappointed, their encounter with the city often inspired them to write down their impressions, which remain irreplaceable documents on the state of Rome in their time.

The Pantheon was built between AD 119 and 128. It is the best-preserved ancient monument in Rome today.

In AD 357 the Emperor Constantius II made a pilgrimage to Rome. A historian of the time, Ammianus Marcellinus, recounts that visit.

As he went on, having entered Rome, that home of sovereignty and of all virtues, when he arrived at the rostra, he gazed with amazed awe on the Forum, the most renowned monument of ancient power; and, being bewildered with the number of wonders on every side to which he turned his eyes, having addressed the nobles in the senate-house, and harangued the populace from the tribune, he retired, with the goodwill of all, into his palace, where he enjoyed the luxury he had wished for.

And often, when celebrating the equestrian games, was he delighted with the talkativeness of the common people, who were neither proud, nor, on the other hand, inclined to become rebellious from too much liberty, while he himself also reverently observed a proper moderation. For he did not, as was usually done in other cities, allow the length of the gladiatorial contests to depend on his caprice; but left it to be decided by various occurrences. Then, traversing the summits of the seven hills, and the different quarters of the city, whether placed on the slopes of the hills or on the level ground, and visiting, too, the suburban divisions, he was so delighted that whatever he saw first he thought the most excellent of all. Admiring the temple of the Tarpeian Jupiter, which is as much superior to other temples as divine things are superior to those of men; and the baths of the size of provinces; and the vast mass of the amphitheatre, so solidly erected of Tibertine stone, to the

Trajan's Markets were the commercial heart of imperial Rome. They also buttressed the Quirinal Hill, undermined by the building of the Forum of Augustus.

top of which human vision can scarcely reach; and the Pantheon with its vast extent, its imposing height, and the solid magnificence of its arches, and the lofty niches rising one above another like stairs, adorned with the images of former emperors; and the temple of the city, and the forum of peace, and the theatre of Pompey, and the odeum, and the racecourse, and the other ornaments of the Eternal City.

But when he came to the Forum of Trajan, the most exquisite structure, in my opinion, under the canopy of heaven, and admired even by the deities themselves, he stood transfixed with wonder, casting his mind over the gigantic proportions of the place, beyond the power of mortal to describe, and beyond the reasonable desire of mortals to rival. Therefore giving up all hopes of attempting anything of this

kind, he contented himself with saying that he should wish to imitate, and could imitate, the horse of Trajan, which stands by itself in the middle of the hall, bearing the emperor himself on his back.

And the royal prince Hormisda, whose departure from Persia we have already mentioned, standing by answered, with the refinement of his nature, 'But first, O Emperor, command such a stable to be built for him, if you can, that the horse on which you purpose to make may have as fair a domain as this which we see.' And when he was asked what he thought of Rome, he said that 'he was particularly delighted with it because he had learned that men died also there.'

Now after he had beheld all these various objects with awful admiration, the emperor complained of fame, as either deficient in power, or else spiteful, because, though it usually exaggerates everything, it fell very short in its praises of the things which are at Rome; and having deliberated for some time what he should do, he determined to add to the ornaments of the city by erecting an obelisk in the Circus Maximus, the origin and form of which I will describe when I come to the proper place.

Ammianus Marcellinus
The Roman History
Translated by C. D. Yonge, 1887

Michel de Montaigne.

'That eagerness for new and unknown things'

Essayist Michel de Montaigne travelled to Italy around 1580.

Thursday, 26th of January, we went to see Mount Janiculum, on the other side of the Tiber, and closely examined the various objects of curiosity there. Among other things, [Montaigne] saw a large bit of old wall, which had come to light two days before. From this elevation you can contemplate, at one view, the whole extent of Rome, which you cannot do near so well from any other point. On leaving this place, he went to the Vatican, to see the statues which stand in niches in the Belvidere, [*sic*] and the fine gallery of paintings that the pope is collecting from all parts of Italy, and which is nearly finished. Somewhere or other in this excursion, he lost his purse and its contents; and he imagined that in giving alms, which he had done two or three times, and the weather being wet and disagreeable, in his hurry to replace his purse it had slipped down his breeches, instead of going into his pocket. Every day, he amused himself with going about and studying every part of Rome in detail. When he first arrived, he had hired a Frenchman for a guide, but this fellow having taken himself off one day in consequence of some pique, M. de Montaigne determined to do without any guide at all, beyond some maps and books that he had bought, and used to read overnight, putting the information he had thus acquired into practical use the next day; and in this way he soon made himself so thoroughly a master...

The Theatre of Marcellus (above) was built in the 1st century to hold twenty thousand people. Below: plan of ancient Rome reconstructed by the topographer Marco Fabio Calvo in 1527.

that he could have guided his guide.

He observed 'that there is nothing to be seen of ancient Rome but the sky under which it rose and stood and the outline of its form; that the knowledge he had of it was altogether abstract and contemplative, no image of it remaining to satisfy the senses; that those who said that the ruins of Rome at least remained, said more than they were warranted in saying; for the ruins of so stupendous and awful a fabric would enforce more honour and reverence for its memory; nothing, he said, remained of Rome but its sepulchre. The world, in hatred of its long domination, had first destroyed and broken in pieces the various parts of this wondrous body; and then, finding that, even though prostrate and dead, its disfigured remains still filled them with fear and hate, they buried the ruin itself; that the few indications of what it had been, which still tottered above its grave, fortune had permitted to remain there, as some evidence of the infinite greatness which so many ages, so many…parricidal blows, and the never-ending conspiracy of the world against it, had not been able entirely to extinguish; but that, in all probability, even the disfigured members that did remain, were the least worthy of all those that had existed, the malignant fury of the enemies of the immortal glory having impelled them to destroy, in the first instance, that which was finest and most worthy of preservation in the imperial city; that the buildings in this bastard Rome, which the moderns were raising upon, or appending to, the glorious structures of the antique world though they sufficed enough to excite the admiration of the present age, yet

seemed to him to bear a close resemblance to nests that the rooks and the swallows construct upon the roofs and walls of the churches in France, which the Huguenots have demolished. Nay, when he considered the space which this tomb occupies, he feared that the real extent even of that was not known, he doubted whether the greater portion of the grave itself had not been

The *Pasquino*, a Greek marble probably representing Menelaus, was discovered in 1501. It was the custom to write satirical comments about those in power on its base.

could not at all comprehend, when he saw the limited space of some of these seven hills, especially the most famous, such as the Capitoline and the Palatine, how they could have held so great a number of buildings as have been ascribed to them. Merely looking at the remains of the Temple of Peace, the site of the Forum Romanum, the ruins of which look like a mighty mountain just fallen asunder, he could hardly understand how two such edifices could stand even on the whole space of the Capitoline hill, yet, besides these, there were on the hill twenty-five or thirty temples, besides a number of private houses. But, in truth, many of the conjectures which one has formed from pictures of the ancient city are not at all borne out when you get there, for even the site has undergone infinite changes; some of the valleys are filled up, even the deepest of them, such, for instance, as the Velabrum, which, on account of its lying so low, was selected as the main sewer of the city, and formed a watercourse, even this has now become as high as the other natural mountains which surround it, and this has solely been done by the gradual agglomeration of the ruins of old Rome; so, the Monte Savello is nothing but the heaped-up ruins of part of the theatre of Marcellus. He fully believed that an ancient Roman, could one be brought back, would not be able to recognize the place. It has more than once happened that, after digging a long way down, the workmen have come to the top of some high column, which still remained standing on its base far beneath. The modern architects never think of looking for any other foundation for their houses than the tops of old buildings, the roofs of

A 17th-century guide pointing out the wonders of ancient and modern Rome.

buried; it appeared to him that the enormous pile which, years ago, was formed merely of such miserable diggings-up, as bits of tiles and broken pots, a pile which had attained the height and size of many natural mountains (for he considered it to be as high as the hill of Gurson, and twice as large), was an express ordinance of fate, to let the world thoroughly understand, by this strange and amazing proof of grandeur, how surpassing was the glory and preeminence of the city against which they had conspired. He said he which ordinarily form the floors of modern cellars, deeming it in no way necessary to make any examination as to the foundation of the old edifice itself, or the stability of its walls; they securely base their own structure upon the ruined tops of the structure below, just as chance has happened to dispose them during the lapse of ages, and here they raise their modern palaces, as firm and safe as if the foundations were solid rocks. There are many whole streets, that stand above the old ones, full thirty feet.'

Michel de Montaigne
Works of Michael de Montaigne
Vol. IV, 1887
Translated by William Hazlitt

Propositions to make one shiver

In Familiar Letters Written in Italy in 1739–40, *by Charles de Brosses (1709–77), one finds a precise description of the state of the Roman*

Early 18th-century engraving of the Colosseum.

SPACCATO E VEDVTA INTERIORE DELL'ANFITEATRO.

ruins at the time and an echo of the tremendous passion they inspired.

Truly, I believe that it is difficult to find oneself for the first time amid the august solitude of the Colosseum and of the Antonine Baths without feeling a slight shiver in one's soul at the sight of the majesty of their ancient forms which were revered and abandoned. The galleries of the exterior walls of the Colosseum still provide shelter to the minor merchants who spread their wares out on poles placed in the holes from which the bronze tenons in the centre of the blocks of stone had been removed, as I told you. Only a semicircle of the external walls is left; it consists of four monumental floors of arcades and columns, with the bottom floor partially buried. It is held up by its own mass, in spite of the little care that is given to it and in spite of the large stones that hang from its sublime cornices; all it needs is a few repairs. There is still a full circle of lower internal galleries, but they are quite dilapidated and have a very sorry appearance. In the arena, which is quite a large oval space, one can hardly make out the form of the tiers of seats which, according to historians, could hold ninety thousand spectators. I have no trouble believing this, since the amphitheatre in Verona, which is only about a third of the size of this one, can hold about thirty thousand. Seeing the amphitheatre of Verona, which has been so well repaired by its inhabitants, the Romans should be ashamed of leaving their amphitheatre in such disorder, especially as it is so vast and famous and as it still has half of its finest parts; this advantage was not shared by the one in Verona, where

Madame de Staël.

practically nothing is left of the outside wall. My plan, for I make many plans, would be to reduce the Colosseum to a semi-amphitheatre, and to demolish the rest of the arches facing the Caelian Hill, to restore the other half to its former shape and to turn the arena into a fine public square. Wouldn't it be better to have half a Colosseum in good condition than to have a whole one in tatters? And is there anything stopping you, my dear Romans, from putting a huge fountain, or even a lake, in the middle of this square, to give yourselves a reminder of your former naval power?

Constantine's triumphal arch with its three gates could be one of the entrances to the square. It has been very successfully repaired in this century; the barbarians had cut all the statues' heads off; new ones have been made for them; the bas-reliefs have been mended, the pieces of marble have been put back together again; in a word, even though this arch is a blend of good and bad taste (for in Constantine's time, the standard of work was low and the good pieces are those of Trajan's Arch, which was destroyed to be reused for this one), it is, today, one of the main antiquities of Rome, and one of the best-preserved ones.

Can you see that poor little round and low carriage-entrance near the Arch of Constantine? Fall prostrate before it, Quintus, for it is the door to what used to be Cicero's house. The place the master of the Roman Republic passed through when returning home, preceded by twelve torchbearers and followed by two thousand Roman warriors, is now only the meagre atrium of some winegrower's house. What about ourselves? The thought is frightening.

Charles de Brosses,
*Familiar Letters Written in Italy
in 1739–40*, 1799

Romantic Rome

Corinne; or, Italy, *by Madame de Staël
(1766–1817), is set in Rome, where its
heroes, Corinne and Oswald, discover the
poetic charm of the ruins.*

Oswald could not weary of feasting his gaze from the elevated point to which Corinne had led him. The study of history can never act on us like the sight of that scene itself. The eye reigns all powerfully over the soul. He now believed in the old Romans, as if he had lived amongst them. Mental recollections are acquired by reading; those of imagination are born of more immediate impressions, such as give life to thought and seem to render us the witnesses of what we learn. Doubtless

Tourists enjoying the Campo Vaccino.

we are annoyed by the modern dwellings that intrude on these wrecks, yet a portico beside some humble roof, columns between which the little windows of a church peep out, or a tomb that serves for the abode of a rustic family, so blends the grand with the simple, and affords us so many agreeable discoveries, as to keep up continual interest. Everything is commonplace and prosaic in the generality of European towns; and Rome, more frequently than any other, presents the sad aspect of misery and degradation; but all at once some broken column or half-effaced bas-relief, or a few stones bound together by indestructible cement, will remind you that there is in man an eternal power, a divine spark, which he ought never to weary of fanning in his own breast, and reluming in those of others. The Forum, whose narrow enclosure has been the scene of so many wondrous events, is a striking proof of man's moral greatness. When in the latter days of Rome, the world was subjected to inglorious rulers, centuries passed from which history could scarce extract a single feat. This Forum, the heart of a circumscribed town, whose natives fought around it against the invaders of its territories – this Forum, by the recollections it retraces, has been the theme of genius in every age. Eternal honours to the brave and free, who thus vanquish even the hearts of posterity.

Corinne observed to Nevil that there were but few vestiges left of the republic, or of the regal day that preceded it. The aqueducts and subterranean canals are the only luxuries remaining while of aught more useful we have but a few tombs and brick temples. Not till after the fall of Sicily did the Romans adopt the use of marble; but it is enough to survey the spots on which great actions have been performed; we experience that indefinite emotion to which we may attribute the pious zeal of pilgrims. Celebrated countries of all kinds, even when despoiled of their great men and great works, exert a power over the imagination. That which would once have attracted the eye exists no more, but the charm of memory still survives.

Madame de Staël
Corinne; or, Italy
Translated by Isabel Hill, 1883

The esthetics of ruins

Historian Jean-Jacques Ampère (1800–64) blended travel writing and historical criticism. 'Criticism has always been slightly provincial,' he writes, 'I wanted to let it see the world.'

The poetic taste for and response to ruins did not exist in the 16th or 17th century. It emerged in France at the end of the 18th century, together with melancholy, which is hardly found in French literature before Rousseau. The century of the senses and of the mind had to arrive at it, for melancholy lies at the end of thought and pleasure. Bernardin de Saint-Pierre had already said some charming things about the grace of ruins; but the person who really revealed their poetic charm was the man who reopened for the new century the realm of religion and of imagination, which the previous century thought it had locked up. In the *Genius of Christianity* readers had been able to admire an eloquent theory of ruins and now, here was the author of that immortal book in Rome, amid the ruins of the imperial city, which had become the great Christian metropolis. How could he fail to find there wonderful words with which to express what they inspired in him? Had he not also learned from events and from life to understand their severe language?... He was doubly prepared by his time and by his genius to feel and to express the grandiose character and the moving melancholy of the Roman ruins. He devoted only a few lines to them in a swift correspondence; but what penetrating precision one finds in the following letter:

'Whoever has no more ties in his life should come to live in Rome; there, he will find for company a land that will inspire his reflections, walks that will always tell him something. The stones he walks over will speak to him, and the dust that the wind will raise under his feet will contain some human greatness.' What follows refers to Hadrian's Villa at Tivoli but describes in a marvellous way the picturesque and melancholy effects that are often reproduced in the ruins of Rome:

'Around me, through the arches of the ruins, vistas of the Roman landscape open up: elder bushes filled the deserted rooms where a few solitary blackbirds sought refuge; the fragments of masonry were carpeted with leaves of scolopendrium, whose green satin stood out like a mosaic upon the marble. Here and there tall cypresses took the place of columns that had fallen in these palaces of death. Wild acanthus crept at their feet over the ruins, as though nature had enjoyed reproducing on these mutilated masterpieces of architecture the decoration of their former beauty; the various rooms and the tops of the ruins looked like baskets and bunches of greenery; the wind ruffled the moist garlands, and the plants bent beneath the rain that fell from the sky.'

But it was not only the ruins themselves whose physiognomy and character were perfectly expressed by the writer. That other poetry of Rome, which is more intimate and which appears only to those who consider it more carefully and with greater love, the poetry of solitary places, of deserted streets, of empty cloisters, that poetry had not been lost to him, and, beside a description of the Colosseum illuminated by the moon, it inspired him to pen the following words; I take them from a letter that is not as well known as the splendid letter to M. de Fontanes.

'Rome sleeps amid its ruins; this star of the night, a globe which one imagines to be finished and depopulated, shines down in its pale solitude on the solitude of Rome; it lights up uninhabited streets, enclosures, squares, gardens that

Antiquity incarnate greets a 19th-century traveller in Rome.

nobody crosses; monasteries in which one no longer hears the monks' voices; cloisters that are as deserted as the porticoes of the Colosseum.'

Jean-Jacques Ampère
Portraits of Rome in Different Ages
1835

Travel notebook

The novelist Emile Zola (1840–1902) journeyed to Rome in 1893.

Spent the whole day in the ruins, an indigestion of ruins, which can evoke the grandeur of Rome. In the morning, first in the Forum. The columns that remain of the Temple of Vespasian, a tremendous effect of elegance and power, against the blue sky. The Basilica Julia, only a trace, but a very clear one, on the ground. The small size of the Forum, which is always surprising when one compares it to certain monuments, the Colosseum, the Baths of Caracalla. It seems that life in Rome was sometimes restricted to very small spaces (Livia's house, etc.) and at other times spread out over considerable areas. Why? Is the problem resolved? Further on, the atrium of the Vestals, the ancient 'convent' of the Vestal Virgins: interesting remains dominated by the ruins of the Palace of Caligula, which descends from the Palatine. Almost directly opposite, a church was placed within a temple of another religion. The red porphyry columns. But the main surprise is the Basilica of Constantine, with its three enormous arches, its three giant coffered vaults; the piece that fell from the vault, an enormous piece. What mass! Why were these walls so gigantic, so thick? From the Via Sacra, which passes in front

of the Basilica of Constantine, one has a very interesting view of the Forum if one turns around. The Via Sacra turns and rises. How the victors must have been shaken on their suspensionless chariots on these rough stones. The present Forum in its ruins, grey and desolate. Dust. Not a patch of grass, a few tufts of grass between the paving stones of the Via Sacra. This with the heavy sun of summer, with the narrow shadows of the few columns still standing, the Column of Phocas and those of the temples. The Arch of Septimius Severus. The rostra, etc. Temples all around. But there are ten ways of reconstructing the Forum. I am only an artist evoking the scene.

Next, I went to the Colosseum. The enormous mass, the collapsed side, the side that's standing with its bays against the blue sky. From everywhere, vaulted corridors that open out, or headless staircases, like slopes. The colossus is like a lacework of stone with all its openings against the blue sky. A blue sky above, very bright, with flights of small clouds…. A ruin baked by the sun, golden, majestic and still gigantic in its half-dilapidated state. The Arch of Titus, with its bas-relief of the defeated Jews brought back as slaves and carrying a menorah.

In the afternoon, I went to the Baths of Caracalla. It is a gigantic and inexplicable building. Two immense vestibules with areas of mosaic paving in good condition. A frigidarium, with marks of a pool in which five hundred people could bathe at one time. Also, a vast tepidarium and a similar caldarium, with a whole system of heating furnaces still visible beside it. As well as all kinds of outbuildings whose use is unknown. But the amazing thing is the height of the rooms, the thickness of the walls, the awesome mass of the monument. None of our medieval castles were built with this Cyclopean mass. Extravagant banks of brick and cement. It must also be said that that was all covered with precious marble and adorned with statues. An overwhelming luxury in size. For what colossal civilization? People walking around it look like ants. Today it all looks like rough stones, materials piled up to form Titans' homes.

Emile Zola
My Journeys: Lourdes, Rome

View of the Via Sacra from the Colosseum (above). Tourists at the Forum at the end of the 19th century (below).

Parker the photographer

*John Henry Parker
(1806–84), an English
publisher and bookseller,
visited Rome in 1863.
Overwhelmed by its ancient
monuments, he founded a
society of archaeology lovers
and organized many lectures
and excursions. Around 1866
Parker began an ambitious
project: to photograph the
major monuments of Rome
systematically. In 1879 he
published the fruits of his
work, a catalogue of about
3300 photographs.*

Remains of the Claudian aqueduct in the
Roman Campagna (above and opposite,
below). Fragments of a temple or tomb found
in 1873 in the Baths of Caracalla (right).

Above left: a display of sculpture. Above right: a view of the church of Santa Croce in Gerusalemme. Below: remains of the Temple of Hadrian.

Above: the Meta Sudans, a fountain in front of the Colosseum, destroyed in the 1930s. Below: the tomb of the Naso family on the Via Flaminia, with now-vanished paintings.

Tales of excavations

The first archaeologists in Rome were treasure hunters. Ancient objects were sought after with the aim of making an instant profit, in terms of money or social prestige. In the first accounts of the excavations, one reads of that greed and the haste to amass objects and to amaze people.

An artist and antiquity

Benvenuto Cellini (1500–71) became famous as a sculptor and goldsmith. Like the other artists of his time, he sketched and surveyed ancient monuments – and took part in the treasure hunt.

At that time, while I was still a young man of about twenty-three, there raged a plague of such extraordinary violence that many thousands died of it every day in Rome. Somewhat terrified at this calamity, I began to take certain amusements, as my mind suggested, and for a reason which I will presently relate. I had formed a habit of going on feast-days to the ancient buildings and modelling parts of them in wax or with the pencil; and since these buildings are all ruins, and the ruins house innumerable pigeons, it came into my head to use my gun against these birds. So then, avoiding all commerce with people, in my terror of the plague, I used to put a fowling-piece on my boy Pagolino's shoulder, and he and I went out alone into the ruins; and oftentimes we came home laden with a cargo of the fattest pigeons. I did not care to charge my gun with more than a single ball; and thus it was by pure skill in the art that I filled such heavy bags. I had a fowling-piece which I had made myself; inside and out it was as bright as any mirror. I also used to make a very fine sort of powder, in doing which I discovered secret processes beyond any which have yet been found; and on this point, in order to be brief, I will give but one particular, which will astonish good shots of every degree. This is, that when I charged my gun with powder weighing one-fifth of the ball, it carried two hundred paces point-blank.

It is true that the great delight I took in this exercise bid fair to withdraw me from my art and studies; yet in another way it gave me more than it deprived me of, seeing that each time I went out shooting I returned with greatly better health, because the open air was a benefit to my constitution. My natural temperament was melancholy, and while I was taking these amusements, my heart leapt up with joy, and I found that I could work better and with far greater mastery than when I spent my whole time in study and manual labour. In this way my gun…

Benvenuto Cellini.

stood me more in profit than in loss.

It was also the cause of my making acquaintance with certain hunters after curiosities, who followed in the track of those Lombard peasants who used to come to Rome to till the vineyards at the proper season. While digging the ground, they frequently turned up antique medals, agates, chrysoprases, cornelians, and cameos; also sometimes jewels, as for instance emeralds, sapphires, diamonds, and rubies. The peasants used to sell things of this sort to the traders for a mere trifle; and very often when I met them, I paid them several times as many golden crowns as they had given *giulios* for some object. Independent of the profit I made by this traffic, which was at least tenfold, it brought me also into agreeable relations with nearly all the cardinals of Rome. I will only touch upon a few of the most notable and rarest of these curiosities. There came into my hands, among many other fragments, the head of a dolphin about as big as a good-sized ballot-bean. Not only was the style of this head extremely beautiful, but nature had here far surpassed art; for the stone was an emerald of such good colour, that the man who bought it from me for tens of crowns sold it again for hundreds after setting it as a finger-ring. I will mention another kind of gem; this was a magnificent topaz; and here art equaled nature; it was as large as a big hazel-nut, with the head of Minerva in a style of inconceivable beauty. I remember yet another precious stone, different from these; it was a cameo, engraved with Hercules binding Cerberus of the triple throat; such was its beauty and the skill of its workmanship, that our great Michel Agnolo [*sic*] protested he

had never seen anything so wonderful.
Among many bronze medals, I
obtained one upon which was a head
of Jupiter. It was the largest that had
ever been seen; the head of the most
perfect execution; and it had on
the reverse side a very fine design of
some little figures in the same style. I
might enlarge at great length on this
curiosity; but I will refrain for fear of
being prolix.

The Life of Benvenuto Cellini,
Translated by John Addington
Symonds, 1888

Find after find

*Flaminio Vacca was an architect who
was passionately interested in antiquities.
His memoirs, the first example of an
account of excavations, are a precious
document about the discoveries of his
time, even if his taste for anecdotes
sometimes takes precedence over the truth.*

I heard Gabriele Vacca, my father,
say that Cardinal della Valle, who
was eager to dig up treasures, had his
workers dig in the Baths of Marcus
Agrippa, where they found a large
imperial Roman gilded crown. As it
resembled a kind of ring cake called
gimbletos, which were sold in the
streets of Rome, the workers said:
'Here is a *gimbleto.*' And hoping
to receive a tip, they rushed to the
cardinal's home and said to him:
'We have found a bronze *gimbleto.*'
The innkeeper who came to live in
that area shortly afterward took this
gimbleto as his sign. That is why it has
always been called the Gimbleto.

My house, the house that I am
presently living in, is built over those
baths. When I wished to build a wall, I
found water. By probing with a metal

bar I found a Corinthian capital. It
measured four spans from the base to
the flower; in this it was identical to the
ones in the portico of the Rotunda.
There was too much water, and I had
to let it rest. When building the cellar, I
found a large niche entirely covered
with flat terra-cotta pipes, which simply
served to conduct heat in this furnace.
Underneath it I found the floor,
covered with slabs of marble, on which
the ancients had walked; under the
slabs there were thick paving stones
and, under those, numerous pillars that
held them up. It was between two of
those pillars that the hearth had been
situated; there were still ashes and
coals there. We also found a large
hole full of sheets of lead, fastened
minutely with nails, and four columns
of granite that were not very tall.
Then I decided to build the wall
without looking further.

I remember that in the street where
the Leutari live, near the Palace of the
Chancellery, in the time of Pope Julius
III they found a statue of Pompey
beneath a cellar; it was fifteen spans
high. There was a wall separating two
houses above its neck. The owner of
one of the houses was told by the other
owner that he could not have it, each of
them believing that he was the owner of
the statue; one of them alleged that,
since he possessed the larger part of it,
it should by right be his; the other said
that it belonged to him because he
had the head, the most important part
of the statue, in his house. Finally, after
all this quarrelling the case went to
court. The judge, an ignorant man,
ordered that the head be broken off and

Section, elevation and plan of the 'Temple of
Peace', by Antoine Desgodets.

I. *Planche*

DV TEMPLE DE LA PAIX, A ROME.

107

Colonne dressée deuant
S.ᵗᵉ Marie Majeure.

Profil sur la largeur.

Profil sur la longeur

Plan de ce qui reste a present.

that each of them should get his share of the statue. Poor Pompey! It had not been enough that Ptolemy had had his head cut off, his bad luck was pursuing him even in his marble state. When Cardinal Capodiferro heard about this stupid judgment, he had it suspended and went to see Pope Julius to tell him the story. The pope was amazed; he immediately ordered that it be carefully dug up for him, and he sent five hundred crowns to the owners for them to share. Once the statue was removed he gave it to the same Cardinal Capodiferro. It was certainly a papal judgment but it took a Capodiferro [Head of Iron] to accomplish. The statue is presently in a room in his palace at the Ponte Sisto.

In my father, Gabriele Vacca's, vineyard, beside the Porta Salaria, inside the walls, there is a piece of land that is called the Gardens of Sallust. When the ground was dug up, they found a large oval building surrounded by a portico adorned with yellow columns; they were eighteen spans tall and fluted, with Corinthian capitals and bases. This oval building had four entrances leading to marble staircases that led down to the level of the floor, made of speckled marbles laid out in beautiful patterns; at each of these entrances there stood two columns of transparent oriental alabaster. Beneath the building, we found a few pipes wide enough for a person to walk through without having to bend over all covered with slabs of Greek marble, as well as two lead pipes ten spans long and each over a span in diameter bearing the following inscription: NERONIS CLAUDIVS. Many medals of Gordian, made of silver and other metals and about the size of small coins, were also

found there, as well as a large quantity of mosaics. The Cardinal of Montepulciano bought the yellow columns and used them in the building of the balustrade of his chapel in San Pietro in Montorio. He also bought the alabaster columns; he had the one that was whole polished and had the others that were broken made into tables, which he sent as a present to the King of Portugal together with other antiquities. But when they were on the high seas, impetuous Fortune, finding them in her domain, made of them a present to the sea.

On the Roman Forum, near the Arch of Septimius, I saw the extraction of great pedestals which are now in the courtyard of Cardinal Farnese; they were covered with letters and names.

B egun in AD 206, the Baths of Caracalla (the ruins
people, this complex contained a gymnasium, a

A few years ago, when I used to go to look at antiquities, I once found myself outside the Porta San Bastiano, at the Capo di Bove, and went into a small inn to shelter from the rain. While I was waiting and talking to the innkeeper, he told me that a few months earlier a man had come there looking for a light; he had come back that evening to have dinner with three friends, with whom he then left. But his three friends never spoke and this went on for six consecutive evenings. The innkeeper began to suspect them, fearing that they might do some evil deed, and he decided to report them. Thus, one evening, when they had just dined as usual, he followed them with the help of the moon and saw them entering some caves in the Circus of Caracalla. The next morning he told the authorities of this and they immediately went there. Looking inside the caves, they found that a large amount of soil had been dug in which there were many pieces of pottery and vases that had only recently been broken. Scratching this soil, they found iron tools that had been used to dig that were now covered over. Wishing to shed some light on the incident and not being far from the spot myself, I went there; I saw piles of earth and the pieces of vases in the shape of jars. It is believed that these men were Goths, who had found this treasure with the help of some ancient piece of information.

Flaminio Vacca
Memoirs, 1704

hich are shown here) were the most sumptuous in Rome. Able to accommodate sixteen hundred tadium, an art gallery, and pleasure gardens.

Extraordinary events

Pietro Santi Bartoli (1635–1700) was passionately interested in Roman architecture. His many attempts at pictorial reconstruction, which prefigure Piranesi's Roman Antiquities, and his drawings of the reliefs of Trajan's Column assured him a reputation as a scholar with a genuine interest in archaeology.

Colosseum

When digging in the garden of a certain Lady dei Nobili, to the north of the Colosseum, we found various underground rooms all nobly decorated with marble, paintings, furniture and statues, as well as a large number of lead pipes, which enabled us to understand that this was a place of leisure that had a certain prestige.

San Gregorio

In the garden of the Cornovaglia, opposite San Gregorio, excavations have been taking place for a long time. Marvellous buildings have been seen there, underground painted rooms, porticoes, immense travertine pillars, statues, baths, busts, and a large quantity of metals; and, among other things, there were a small iron box containing all the instruments of sacrifice and a porphyry lion that was sold to Cardinal Chigi. But what seemed most remarkable was a room approximately twelve spans long, whose floor was covered with lead, which was raised at the level of the walls by about one span. Between this lead and the wall, where it had come slightly loose, we found a large number of gold coins; we thought that this might be the treasury of the empire or the fortune of a great personage.

Digging began again in the same place [the garden of Francesco Morelli on the Caelian] at the time of Clement X, and remains were found there of the most beautiful paintings to have been seen in Rome, as well as various statues and some very fine busts, especially the two *Lucius Verus* purchased by Cardinal di Buglione, as well as *Eros* and *Psyche*, bought by the Cardinal de' Medici, not to mention various other statues of speckled marble, a very fine metal lamp representing the ship of St Peter, and various other very fine antiquities.

Opposite this spot…they attempted to extract a treasure, but they were disappointed to find only a large number of bronze coins whose value was only that of their weight as old metal. Later, in the time of Innocent X, digging began at the level of the lower gate, leading to the alley that goes to the Colosseum, and they discovered a row of shops that seemed to have been used by coppersmiths, as there were a large number of pieces of copper there, together with the tools used to work them. Because of this and out of respect for the noble neighbourhood, the excavations were ended there. They were restarted at the time of Clement X, and part of the building called Castra Peregrina was found there, in addition to some fine salt storage rooms, courtyards with their porticoes, columns made of a very beautiful breccia which were reused for the mortuary chapel of the church of San Lorenzo fuori le Mura, statues, a large number of marble heads, countless busts and metal fragments, some of which had doubtless been used for a triumphal arch, many of them being plated and encrusted with silver….

Antoniana (Baths of Caracalla)

The discovery of the Farnese Hercules was an extraordinary event: the body was found at the Antoniana, the head at the bottom of a well in the Trastevere, which was being cleared, and, last, the legs were found at Frattocchie, not far from Marino, where excavations had taken place. Today, these legs may be seen in the cellars of the Villa Borghese, among other antiquities.

The excavations that took place in the Antoniana at the time of Pope Paul III, on the orders of Cardinal Farnese, his grandson, unearthed such a profusion of statues, columns, bas-reliefs, various speckled marbles, not to mention a large number of small objects, metal statuettes, medals, oil lamps, and other similar objects, that this prince's palace became a wonderful place, as it still is today. For it alone can boast of having colossi of such an excellent style as the two *Hercules*, as well as the *Flora*, the *Gladiators*, and other statues, including that marvellous composition, the *Bull*, of stupendous size, and a large number of statues made of a single piece of marble or the countless heads, busts, and bas-reliefs that still remain heaped up, as if in storage, in two vast rooms on the ground floor. All of this, or the greater part of it, was found at the Antoniana, apart from the bas-reliefs in the outer courtyard where the *Bull* stands, which were found in the Piazza di Pietra, where the eleven great Corinthian columns of the portico called the Basilica of Antoninus can still be seen today [this monument is now identified as the Temple of Hadrian, 2nd century AD]. A portion of the marbles that were found there was discovered in the time of Innocent X, when water pipes were being connected to the fountain of the Piazza Navona; others were found during demolition of a church in order to give the place to be used by all the secondhand dealers of the Rotunda a more majestic appearance; Pope Alexander VII wanted this to be done in order to give the imposing temple a more noble character by opening up one's view of it. A few houses that were crowding in on the temple's portico were demolished, and in doing this, in the walls of that portico, they found similar statues representing Provinces [statues belonging to the Temple of Hadrian], filling the spaces between the columns; the best-preserved of these were then placed on the staircases of the palace of the cardinal, his nephew. Those that were found in the time of Innocent were fastened to the facade of the palace in his villa outside the Porta San Pancrazio. Others were placed on the Capitol.

Pietro Santi Bartoli,
*Memoirs of Various Excavations Made
in Rome and Surrounding Areas,*
17th century

A drawing by Bartoli of a building discovered in 1683.

The French in Rome

François-René de Chateaubriand, a diplomat, acutely observed the effects of the French administration in Rome.

The first invasion of Rome by the French, under the Directorate, was infamous and accompanied by plunder; the second, under the Empire, was iniquitous: but once accomplished, order reigned.

The Republic demanded of Rome, for an armistice, twenty-two million francs, the occupation of the Citadel of Ancona, one hundred pictures and statues, and one hundred manuscripts, to be selected by the French commissaries. They especially wanted to have the busts of Brutus and Marcus Aurelius: so many people in France called themselves Brutus in those days, it was very simple that they should wish to possess the pious image of their putative father; but Marcus Aurelius – whose father was he? Attila, to go away from Rome, asked only a certain number of pounds of pepper and silk: In our day, Rome for a moment redeemed her liberty with pictures. Great artists, often neglected and unhappy, left their masterpieces to serve as a ransom for the ungrateful cities that slighted them.

The Frenchmen of the Empire had to repair the ravages the Frenchmen of the Republic had committed in Rome; they also owed a debt for the sack of Rome accomplished by an army led by a French prince: It was fitting that Bonaparte should set order in the ruins that another Bonaparte had seen grow, and whose overthrow he described. The plan adopted by the French Administration for the excavation of

the Forum was that which Raphael proposed to Leo X: it caused to rise from the earth the three columns of the Temple of Concord; it exposed the pavement of the Via Sacra; it did away with the new buildings with which the Temple of Peace was encumbered; it removed the soil that covered the steps of the Colosseum, cleared the interior of the arena, and brought to view seven or eight rooms in the Baths of Titus.

Elsewhere, the Forum of Trajan was explored, the Pantheon, the Baths of Diocletian, and the Temple of Patrician Modesty repaired. Funds were put aside for the maintenance, outside Rome, of the Walls of Falerii and the Tomb of Caecilia Metella.

Repair work was also undertaken for modern edifices: St. Paul's Without the Walls, which no longer exists, had its roofing repaired; St. Agnes' and San Marino ai Monti were protected against the weather. A portion of the roof and the pavement of St. Peter's was mended; lightning rods shielded the dome of Michael Angelo from the lightning. The sites were marked out of two cemeteries in the east and west of the city, and that on the east, near the Convent of San Lorenzo, was finished.

The Quirinal arrayed its external poverty in the luxury of porphyry and Roman marbles: Designed as it was for the imperial palace, Bonaparte, before taking up his residence there, wanted to remove all traces of the abduction of the pontiff held captive at Fontainebleau. It was proposed to pull down the part of the city lying between the Capitol and Monte Cavallo, so that the triumphant might ride up to his Caesarian abode through an immense avenue; events caused these gigantic dreams to fade away by destroying enormous realities.

Among the plans decided was that of building a series of quays from Ripetta to Ripa Grande: the foundations of those quays would have been laid; the four blocks of houses between the Castle of Sant' Angelo and the Piazza Rusticucci were partly bought up and would have been demolished. A wide thoroughfare would thus have been seen from the foot of the Castle of Sant' Angelo.

The French make walks wherever they go: At Cairo, I have seen a great square, which they had planted with palm trees and surrounded with cafés bearing names borrowed from the cafés of Paris; in Rome, my fellow-countrymen created the Pincio; you reach it by a flight of stairs....

The western portion of the Piazza del Popolo was to have been planted in the space occupied by work-yards and shops; from the end of the open place

Picturesque view of archaeologists at work in the Forum, c. 1820.

Sarcophagi, urns and funerary stelae discovered in 1775 near a vineyard.

one would have seen the Capitol, the Vatican and St. Peter's beyond the quays of the Tiber: in other words, ancient and modern Rome.

The Memoirs of François-René Vicomte de Chateaubriand, Translated by Alexander Teixeira de Mattos, 1902

A German in Rome

The author of the long History of Medieval Rome, *Ferdinand Gregorovius (1821–91), moved to Rome on the eve of Italian unification.*

18 June 1871

Rome has become a whitewashed sepulchre. The houses, and even the ancient and revered palaces, are coated with white; the rust of centuries is scraped away, and we now see, for the first time, how architecturally ugly Rome really is. Rosa has shaved even the Colosseum – that is to say, has cleared away all the plants that made it so beautiful. The Flora of the Colosseum, on which Deakin, an Englishman, wrote a book some years ago, has thus been destroyed. This transformation of the sacred city into a secular, is the reverse of the time when, with a like enthusiasm, pagan Rome transformed herself into a spiritual city. The convents are being turned into offices; the barred windows are opened, or new doors broken in the walls. After long centuries, sun and air again penetrate into these cells of monks and nuns. Thus within a short space of time St. Silvestro, the convent of the Philippines, the Minerva, the Augustinian in the [Campus Martius], the Apostolic Saints, have undergone a violent transformation. The monks who dwelt there are hounded out like

badgers; it is a piteous sight to behold them stealing about ghostlike through their rooms, cloisters, and corridors. Some must rejoice at the prospect of being so soon released from their ban. Ancient Rome is fading. In the course of twenty years the world here will be a new one.

12 January 1873

Building is proceeding at a furious pace; the Monti quarter is turned entirely upside-down. Yesterday saw the fall of the lofty walls of the Villa Negroni; streets are being laid out even there; a new quarter of the city is already rising on the Praetorian Camp, another on the slopes of the Coelian beside the Quattro Coronati. Building is also going on beside St. Lorenzo in Paneperna. Almost every hour witnesses the fall of some portion of ancient Rome. New Rome belongs to the new generation, while I belong to the ancient city, in whose spellbound silence my history arose. Were I to come to Rome now for the first time, I neither should nor could conceive the idea of such a work....

2 April 1874

The convents are now almost all suppressed and deserted. Went one evening to St. Onofrio, the very eve of the day on which the monks were to evacuate the building. On entering the cloisters, saw some of them sitting silent and sad round the stone fountain; storm-clouds hung over the Janiculum, throwing the convent into shadow; the lightning flashed, and there were peals of thunder.

A Roman National Museum has been erected in St. Lorenzo in Lucina. The fate of other convents remains as

Excavating the Forum at the end of the 19th century.

yet undecided. The State archives are to be removed to the house of the Greek Basilians of S. Maria in the [Campus Martius]. The Armenians on the height beside [St Peter's] in Vincoli keep a school, and have, consequently, been allowed to retain their quarters. But a Polytechnic Institution has fixed its abode in the monastery of [St Peter's] itself.

In the Augustinian Monastery and at the Minerva the monks have remained on as librarians. Have not yet visited either of these libraries where for years I felt myself so much at home, and where I was always greeted with the same friendliness. Now that my name is on the Index, I do not wish to see the astonished faces of the good old men; am pained to think that many people must form unjust ideas about me, ideas that I am unable to remove.

The excavations in the Colosseum proceed apace; huge subterranean canals are brought to light. Nothing important in the way of statues has been discovered. In order to make these excavations, all the chapels of the Stations and also the Cross in the middle have been removed. This proceeding aroused a storm on the part of all the pious and in the Vatican. The Cardinal Vicar laid the Director Rosa under the ban; processions daily wound their way to the Colosseum to pray. Digging was industriously carried on.

Ferdinand Gregorovius,
The Roman Journals,
Translated by Mrs Gustavus
Hamilton, 1911

Christian archaeology

The discovery of the catacombs shed a great deal of new light on the funerary rites of the Early Christians. With the increasingly active assistance of the pontifical authorities, underground Rome was gradually revealed. Between 1939 and 1949 Pius XII had a search made for the tomb of St Peter beneath the basilica. The excavations revealed an ancient necropolis and the outline of a Roman road.

A visit to the catacombs

If one is to believe the scholar Charles de Brosses (1709–77), there was little interest in the catacombs in the 18th century. In any case, only a few of the tombs were known, and it was not really possible to visit them. The Catacombs of St Sebastian, for example, were a bandits' lair.

Charles de Brosses.

From one extreme to the other, I shall drop you into the catacombs; this will save you the trouble of seeing those of Rome, for these are not objects that are of interest more than once. And yet, I was foolish enough to visit those of St Agnes, but may my example make you wise. They are long underground corridors dug into stone quarries. On each side, the stone is cut into niches, like a library.

It may be stated with certainty that

Cubicolo Primo del Cimiterio di S. Califto Papa, e d'altri Santi Martiri nelle Vie Appia, & Ardeatina.

CVBICVLVM PRIMVM
COEMETERII SANCTI CALLISTI PAPAE
ET ALIORVM SANCTORVM MARTYRVM
VIA APPIA ET ARDEATINA

Chambers in the Catacombs of St Callistus drawn by Bosio for his book *Underground Rome*.

this was never done for any other reason than to be used as a cemetery, either since the custom of burning bodies had been abandoned, or perhaps even before that custom was introduced; at least, one might think that of the catacombs of Rome. One or more bodies were laid in each niche, after which it seems to have been sealed up in order to prevent infection. It is ridiculous and foolish to claim that they were dug by the first Christians in order to live in them and to celebrate the sacred mysteries, protected from persecution.

What fine lodgings such tunnels would make, deprived as they are of air and of light! It would be a truly fine project to have accomplished *incognito*

this whole series of wide and high corridors, a labyrinth of tunnels covering at least nine miles [14 km].

There were not enough Christians in Naples to undertake, even publicly, a project such as their catacombs, which are finer and less deep than those of Rome. I would agree that, occasionally, by chance, somebody might have hidden in them; but they were certainly never a home for the living. The remains of altars and of paintings daubed on the walls, which can be seen in quite a large room at the entrance to the catacombs of Naples, are apparently the marks of some pious ceremony which used to take place there in honour of the dead saints who were thought to have lived there.

That is all I am prepared to tell you on the subject; if you want to know more, read Misson and Burnet, who have a lot to say about it.

Charles de Brosses
Sensations of Italy
18th century

Cemetery of St Callistus

Giovanni Battista de' Rossi discovered the Catacombs of St Callistus in 1849 and was the founder of Christian archaeology. His book Underground Christian Rome *was not only a scholarly study but an exciting account of his adventures in the depths of the earth.*

Crypt of St Cornelius

In 1849 in the Molinari vineyard, which today is the property of the Holy Apostolic Palaces, I discovered a fragment of a marble plaque engraved with fine letters, on which part of the name of St Cornelius was still inscribed: …RNELIVS MARTYR. This fragment seemed to me to belong to the epitaph that had once been placed over the sepulchre of St Cornelius. I showed it to Father Marchi, who acquired it for the Museum Kircherianum.

Four years later, on a day in March 1852,…I walked with Father Marchi to the end of the northern corridor, which was partly blocked with soil, so that we had to bend down as we walked under the vault.

At the end we found a hole that had recently been dug in the tufa. Putting our heads into the hole, we saw a room full, not of soil piled up by gravediggers, but of rubble fallen from above; faced with this, the modern plunderers, following their custom, had retreated without digging a broader

hole. My readers already know what a favourable sign that is. Contemporary research is different from older methods in that we look for precisely those places that lie buried under the rubble fallen from openings, stairs, or ruins of buildings that transformed the original tomb, whereas the plunderers, when they stumbled upon such places, retreated and followed the direction of the excavation made in the tufa and in soil deposits by the gravediggers of ancient times.

The event lived up to our hopes.

First to appear was an arch built of good bricks, a sure sign of transformations and restorations of the early crypt. Then, beneath the arch, we

Fragments of Christian inscriptions found in the catacombs (above). Ceremony in a catacomb in the 19th century (opposite).

discovered paintings; they were pictures of two saints in Byzantine style, the incontrovertible sign that this was a famous and historic crypt. There was an inscription beside the first painting: SCI CORNELI PP, and beside the second one: ...IPPI...N...

Readers remembering what I said about St Cyprian, whose cult was associated with that of St Cornelius, will immediately be able to complete and read the second name: CIPRIANI. Here, therefore, were Cornelius and Cyprian in a historic crypt in the cemetery of Callistus, not far from that of St Sixtus and St Cecilia.

How can one doubt that this was the very tomb of St Cornelius himself, about which topographers have given us so much precise information?

As for me, hardly had I seen the pictures than I was overcome with an incredible joy (it was the first time that I had found myself in the underground cemeteries in front of a pope's funerary monument), and I did not ask myself whether the tomb next to this painting was really the one that I imagined.

On the other side of the tomb itself we saw the effigies of two other saints in their priestly robes: the name of the first one was complete: SCS XYSTVS PP ROM; the second one's name had worn away. The tomb that was flanked by these pictures was open and without any trace of the stone or of the inscription that had once covered it. A few letters of the period of Pope Damasus appeared on a piece of marble that had remained affixed to the right angle above the opening of the tomb.

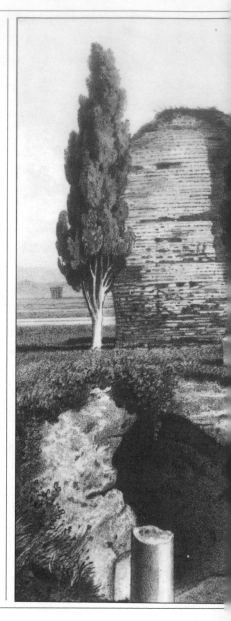

Entrance to a catacomb on the Appian Way.

There was also a small fragment of a long inscription in front of the sarcophagus; it was monumental in its form and proportions and was almost Damasene in its calligraphy. Neither fragment contained a syllable that could suggest a proper name.

What was missing from the lettering surviving on the tomb was found on a third fragment discovered right inside the tomb itself. When this fragment was put next to the one I had found in the vineyard four years earlier, it fitted exactly and thus gave the full inscription: CORNELIVS MARTYR EPiscopus...

The venerable and inestimable title put back together in this way, with two pieces that were discovered at different times, together with a third piece that formed the upper edge of the marble plaque, on which there were no letters, when placed on top of the tomb covered it exactly.

The plaque's thickness proves conclusively that it once formed the lid of this sepulchre; in the left corner of the tomb, one can still see, in the chalk, the mark of this precise thickness.

Giovanni Battista de' Rossi
Underground Christian Rome
1864–77

Christian archaeology: a summing-up

In spite of its youth, Christian archaeology already has quite an impressive history. Philippe Pergola, a French professor of topography at the Pontifical Commission for Christian Archaeology, describes the evolution that has occurred in the methods and objectives of this science, 'which studies the archives of Early Christianity'.

Has Christian archaeology changed much in the 20th century?

Christian archaeology today is no longer the same as that of Antonio Bosio or of Giovanni Battista de' Rossi, but it is its heir and it is proud of this parentage.

The world of Christian archaeology, like that of archaeology as a whole, brings together scholars with differing approaches: art historians, epigraphers, specialists in literary sources, and excavators with 'traditional' methods (including techniques that are criticized today) or the most recent techniques (for example, the 'open area' excavation perfected by British researchers).

Traditionally, Christian archaeology has concerned itself with Christian monuments from late antiquity and the early Middle Ages, especially churches, baptisteries, monasteries and cemeteries; but today its field of investigation has been extended to society as a whole, including economy and politics.

One thus speaks increasingly of archaeology of late antiquity and the early Middle Ages rather than 'Christian archaeology'. In earlier times this discipline concerned itself with monuments up to the start of the 7th century AD (the end of Gregory the Great's pontificate); today, we go right up to the 9th century, if not later.

All the countries of the Western world that became Christian at the end of antiquity and at the beginning of the Middle Ages do certainly have their specialists in Christian archaeology today, but with a very few exceptions, all their activity has a link with Rome and its traditional institutions: notably, the Pontifical Commission for

Christian Archaeology, which has, since the mid-19th century, supervised the excavation and administration of the Roman catacombs, and the Pontifical Institute of Christian Archaeology, founded in 1925, which accepts students from all over the world, who go there for three years to prepare a doctorate in their special field.

What are the great discoveries and the great debates of the last thirty years in this field?

It is almost impossible to list them. Many monuments have been excavated, and their discovery has often cast doubts on firmly entrenched beliefs. To focus on Rome only and the domain of the catacombs, several theories have been overturned, thanks especially to the renewal of scientific study and problematics.

In Rome the most spectacular discovery was that of a catacomb on the Via Latina that was richly decorated with particularly unusual paintings. Besides biblical images, which were totally unknown in this form or were very unusual when compared to the hundreds of other cycles known until now in the Roman catacombs, the owners of these private series had also had entirely pagan scenes painted.

This complex, which may be dated roughly between AD 330 and 380, is the proof, contrary to all expectations on the part of the archaeologists and historians of late antiquity, of a definite tolerance and of a close union, up to and beyond death, between Christians and pagans.

As for the catacombs themselves, recent studies have made it possible to establish that they were not originally specifically Christian but that, in fact, independent of all religious affiliation, they were resorted to systematically, in the early decades, and that this type of burial inside underground tunnels was universal.

Finally, in the last thirty years, Christian archaeology has swelled its ranks and its field of action with the help of stratigraphic excavations carried out by the researchers of the most recent generation; these 'fine' excavations have often made it possible to revise the chronology of a number of monuments, but they have also given us a different image of the end of antiquity and of the early Middle Ages: there was no break caused by the invasions of bloodthirsty barbarians; instead there was a long transition to the Middle Ages, with progressive changes in every domain. The Lombards, for example, were rehabilitated thirty years ago; the Vandals are also now being rehabilitated: their arrival in Africa did not break any of the traditional economic circuits, and the destruction caused by their passing or by their settling in certain provinces now appears only in the writings of those nostalgic for outdated theories that are unequivocally contradicted by all the archaeological discoveries of the last few years.

FURTHER READING

Ammianus Marcellinus, *The Roman History*, trans. C. D. Yonge, 1887

Andreae, Bernard, *The Art of Rome*, 1977

Bianchi Bandinelli, Ranuccio, *Rome: The Centre of Power*, 1970

——, *Rome: The Late Empire*, 1971

Boëthius, Axel, *The Golden House of Nero*, 1960

Gibbon, Edward, *The Decline and Fall of the Roman Empire*, 1776–88/1932

Grabar, André, *Early Christian Art*, 1968

Gregorovius, Ferdinand, *The Roman Journals*, trans. Mrs Gustavus W. Hamilton, 1911

Krautheimer, Richard, *Early Christian and Byzantine Architecture*, 1975

Lanciani, Rodolfo, *The Destruction of Ancient Rome*, 1967

L'Orange, H. P., *Art Forms and Civic Life in the Late Roman Empire*, 1965

MacKendrick, Paul, *The Mute Stones Speak: The Story of Archaeology in Italy*, 1960

McKay, A. G., *Houses, Villas, and Palaces in the Roman World*, 1975

Pollitt, J. J., *The Art of Rome c. 753 BC–AD 337, Sources and Documents*, 1966

Potter, Timothy, *Roman Italy*, 1987

Ramage, Nancy and Andrew, *Roman Art: Romulus to Constantine*, 1991

Salmon, E. T., *The Making of Roman Italy*, 1982

Simon, Erika, *Ara Pacis Augustae*, 1967

Toynbee, J. M. C., *Death and Burial in the Roman World*, 1971

Ward-Perkins, John B., *Roman Architecture*, 1977

Wheeler, R. E. M., *Roman Art and Architecture*, 1964

LIST OF ILLUSTRATIONS

CHAPTER 4

CHAPTER 5

CHAPTER 6

DOCUMENTS

INDEX

ACKNOWLEDGMENTS

The author wishes to thank Filippo Coarelli and Alain Borer for reading the manuscript; Noëlle de la Blanchardière for her advice and encouragement; and Claude Nicolet and Charles Pietri for their kind assistance. Thanks also go to those individuals and organizations who helped with the realization of this work: Annie Coarelli, bookseller in Rome; Philippe Morel, art historian at the Villa Medici; Fausto Zevi, director of the Institute of Art History and Archaeology in Rome; Pierre Pinon, architect; and Nicole Thirion, translator, Editions Robert Laffont

PHOTO CREDITS

TEXT CREDIT

Acknowledgment is made for use of material from Gibbon, Edward, *The Decline and Fall of the Roman Empire*, vol. III, The Modern Library, New York, 1932. The publishers are grateful to the estate of Edward Gibbon and to Chatto & Windus, London.

Claude Moatti, PhD,
teaches at the Sorbonne in Paris. She studied
classics at the Ecole Normale Supérieure in Sèvres,
France, where she specialized in political thought
and the crisis in culture that arose at the end of the
Roman Republic and in the early Roman Empire
(2nd century BC to 1st century AD). A former
member of the staff of the French School in
Rome, Dr Moatti is now doing research on
the history of the discovery of ancient Rome
and the 'invention' of Roman archaeology.
In this book she presents the first
findings of her project.

For Thomas

© 1989 Gallimard
English translation © Thames and Hudson Ltd., London
and Harry N. Abrams, Inc., New York, 1993

Translated by Anthony Zielonka

Printed and bound in Italy
by Editoriale Libraria, Trieste